NATURAL GRACE

Also by William Dietrich

NON-FICTION

Northwest Passage: The Great Columbia River

The Final Forest: The Battle for the

Last Great Trees of the Pacific Northwest

✤

FICTION

Dark Winter

Getting Back

Ice Reich

NATURAL GRACE

The Charm, Wonder, and Lessons
of Pacific Northwest Animals and Plants

William Dietrich

DRAWINGS BY BRENDA CUNNINGHAM

UNIVERSITY OF WASHINGTON PRESS

SEATTLE & LONDON

Copyright © 2003 by the University of Washington Press
Printed in the United States of America
Designed by Audrey Seretha Meyer

Library of Congress Cataloging-in-Publication Data

Dietrich, William, 1951–
Natural grace : the charm, wonder, and lessons of Pacific Northwest
animals and plants / William Dietrich ;
drawings by Brenda Cunningham.
p.   cm.
ISBN 0-295-98293-4 (alk paper)
1. Natural history—Northwest, Pacific.   I. Title
QH104.5.N6 D54   2003
508.795—dc21   2002035977

The paper used in this publication is acid-free and recycled from
10 percent post-consumer and at least 50 percent pre-consumer
waste. It meets the minimum requirements of American National
Standard for Information Sciences—Permanence of Paper for
Printed Library Materials, ANSI z39.48-1984.

Proceeds from this book are donated to environmental education
and conservation organizations.

To the people who fight to conserve

the Northwest environment

❧

CONTENTS

NATURAL GRACE

INTRODUCTION

YOU ANIMAL, YOU.
Please don't take offense. I'm well aware we humans pride ourselves on our obvious differences from the creatures around us. Genesis concludes with people as the finishing touch, flawed but still at the top of the heap. The scientific name for our species is *Homo sapiens sapiens*, which translates from the Latin as "wise, wise us." Accordingly we say we struggle to curb base instincts, to avoid barnyard manners, to rise above animal behavior.

Well. What do animals have to say about *that*?

I hope the essays in this book help persuade you that if actions speak louder than words, animals—and even plants—are eloquent on this subject, demonstrating in all their variety an easy self-possession, nobility, natural grace, hardiness, ingenuity, and endurance we would do well to match. Some animals are beautiful, some comic, and some pitiless from our point of view, but all have that elusive star quality we call *presence*: the integrity of having evolved to fill their niches in nature, to be comfortable in their roles. Can many of us say the same? After all, we humans are animals too. To be compared to the creatures with which we share the planet might just help us to *become* wise, if we can learn to take a broader, more generous point of view.

Our rapidly changing view of nature is the unspoken theme of this collection of natural history essays, adapted from articles first published in the *Pacific Northwest* magazine of the Sunday *Seattle Times*. Even as progress separates us from nature, there is increasing interest in relearning our connection to, and our dependence on, the natural world. The topic is timely. At no point in history has our ethic toward our fellow creatures been more critically important than at the dawn of the twenty-first century.

Why? Because we, and nature, are victims of our own species' spectacular success. The world's human population has increased sixfold in the last two hundred years. Here in the Pacific Northwest the increase is more than one hundredfold. These numbers, coupled with technology and urban growth, have produced the greatest environmental change in this region since the last Ice Age.

The good news is that we humans are physically better off and have more opportunity than at any time in human history. The bad news is that a third of our wetlands, more than half of our marine estuaries and most of our lowland old-growth forest and sage steppe desert is gone. More than a hundred salmon stocks—runs of a particular river with a distinct genetic imprint—are already extinct, and many of the surviving stocks are on the endangered species list. Other saltwater species from herring to hake to rockfish have collapsed in numbers. Shellfish beaches have closed due to pollution. We've introduced hundreds of species both useful and noxious, paved more land than we've saved as cathedral-grove old growth, and planted more trees than we've chopped. We've gardened, cut, sprayed, fertilized, plowed, gouged, and healed. And at the rate of growth experienced in the year 2000, the Pacific Northwest will add the population equivalent of a new city of Seattle or Portland every three years. Every three years! We've come to regard such growth as normal, inevitable. Yet it poses a critical question. Having conquered nature in the Pacific Northwest, can we still coexist with it? How do we conserve the natural world that drew us to the region in the first place?

This is not an environmental policy book. I have no quick, glib answers for a topic so complex that it goes to the very root of our civilization and its assumptions. Rather, it's an awareness book, arguing that we risk losing something profoundly worthwhile. Its point is not that animals and trees are necessarily lovable but simply that they're interesting, and because of that, their lives add immeasurably to our own. I suggest that one useful thing we can do with *our* lives is work toward saving *theirs*.

As traditional Northwest occupations such as farming, fishing, and logging employ a shrinking percentage of our population, the whole notion of what it means to be a Pacific Northwesterner has become fuzzy. Many of us have become tourists to our own landscape, weekend outdoorsmen no longer dependent on working the land to make a living. Comfort has drained us of pioneer color. Globalization is robbing us of regional distinction. In retrospect there's a certain historical inevitability to all this—the homogenization of global culture has gone hand in hand with the acceleration of technology for three hundred years—and nostalgia for the past runs the risk of not only being myopic in its selective memory but pointless, even pathetic. There was little romance in the polluting plumes of long-gone wigwam sawdust burners. There is little regret that most now escape the chainsaw "white finger" and other physical debilitations of outdoor occupations, little complaint that hydroplanes and rodeos are no longer the premier sports events in this fourth corner of the United States. And yet. . . .

With the explosive growth of this region has come an insidious loss of our sense of place. During our short recorded history, what has made the Pacific Northwest distinctive is mountain and Sound, tree and trail, river and range. Yet this Pacific Northwest is increasingly a place that most of us have to drive miles to find. Time pressures add anxiety. Species have to be spotted in an afternoon or not at all. Nature seems more remote, more mysterious, more romantic, more misunderstood.

That's my story, anyway. As a newspaper reporter and author I've spent too much time writing about the environment and not enough experiencing it. Which helps explain the origin of this admittedly self-indulgent book.

I was born and raised in Washington State and have watched its population more than double in my lifetime. Like many Northwest natives I've grumped with dismay about the disappearance of old-growth forest, the collapse of salmon runs, the clogging of highways, the crowding of campgrounds, and the escalation of housing prices. Yet I was a Tacoma kid who knew little about the landscape where I fished, hunted, and hiked. It was green, and pretty, and I was all for the Environment, with a capital E, but it was something to be crossed instead of inhabited, a weekend destination instead of home. I hardly knew and didn't care which tree was which, or what kinds of lives animals might lead. The outdoors was scenery, background, wallpaper for an urban life.

This began to change with age, observation, and my own experiences as a journalist. Witnessing the eruption of Mount

St. Helens in 1980 while I was working at the *Vancouver Columbian* upset any assumptions I had about the permanence of nature. Encounters with rural poverty and the decline of fishing and logging cured me of excessive back-to-the-land romanticism. Clearcuts, pollution, and plug-ugly development convinced me that wise, wise us could be a bunch of wise guys of blind and bullying ambition. Coverage of the environment and science for the *Seattle Times* introduced me to scientists who viewed the same landscapes I did with a completely different level of understanding. The more I learned, the more I realized how ignorant I was. Here was an outdoor world fluid with change, intricate in its Byzantine alliances and rivalries, cruel and magnificent, funny and tragic, monogamous and faithless, cyclic and yet never entirely predictable. And the more I learned, the more I had a jarring sense of unexpected self-recognition. Again and again these plants and animals reminded me of . . . me . . . you . . . us.

Eating. Reproduction. Rivalry. Territory. Succession. Opportunism. Nesting. Here were office and grocery store, career and courtship, restless travel and cozy home, human society in all its instinctual beginnings.

This is not to say that humans are merely animals (or that animals are as complicated and nasty as people can be). We people are unusual in our social systems and global dispersal, and we have a peculiarly restless intellect that clearly sets us apart, for better and worse.

What I *am* saying is that understanding nature is useful for understanding ourselves; that our office politics, hapless romances, adolescent angst, ambitions, vanities, fears, and longings have some parallels in the life cycles of the natural world. People, we are taught in the news business, are primarily interested in people. If so, the creatures around us offer a different way of looking at ourselves. Why else do we go to zoos but for the partial shock of self-recognition?

Additionally, we only care about what we know. We only safeguard what we fear could be lost. As a writer trying to write something useful about the environment, I've concluded that enthusiasm and commitment begin from learning just how marvelous this place is: Passion has to precede purpose.

In my introduction to the series in *Pacific Northwest* magazine, I wrote: "Our intent is celebration, not a sermon. We want to inspire determined optimism, not nostalgic regret." That's still true. No matter what your environmental politics, I hope you find these neighbors of ours both instructive and entertaining. I hope your relationship with them is joyful, not guilty or annoyed. Such coexistence is not always simple. Like any neighbors, animals and plants can sometimes be intrusive or pesky. Nonetheless, good and patient stewardship is vastly simpler than trying to get back to Eden once it is lost.

So, the first step in taking care is caring, and the first step to caring is knowing. Dip into these stories at will, read them in any order, and supplement them with a good field guide, please. I hope to make you laugh a few times, not weep.

And, I hope to encourage you to expand your curiosity beyond the most obvious and famous creatures. The seductive sirens of the natural world are what wildlife biologists wryly call "charismatic megafauna." Nature's celebrities are big, glamorous creatures that people get excited about— eagles, cougars, whales, and the like. The last section of this book looks at these stars. In nature, however, such animals are often bit players in an ecological opera dominated by plant and animal species so common, so important, and so unglamorous that we often hardly notice them. Accordingly, the first section of this book focuses on species so ubiquitous as to be taken for granted. Part Two explores a few of the microscopic or tiny creatures that matter immensely, and Part Three surveys some of the natural processes of weather and geology that influence us and the creatures that live here.

All, of course, are reflections of the greater whole. I hope the following essays encourage you to learn more. And then, I hope you go outside and work to protect this beautiful, marvelous, and fragile corner of the world.

TAKEN FOR
GRANTED

Jellyfish

THERE ARE UNQUESTIONABLY BEAUTIFUL animals in the Pacific Northwest such as the swallowtail butterfly, and lordly ones like the bull elk. There are graceful creations like the great blue heron. There are just plain homely animals such as the ratfish, or slimy residents such as the slug, or stinky ones like the skunk. But there's one group of creatures that is so ethereal, so unworldly, so bizarre, and so elegant as to call into question all our assumptions about beauty—not to mention purpose, menace, and importance.

I refer to the annual bloom of billions upon billions of jellyfish. Here is a reminder of the dawn of life, pulsating like slow breath to some unheard evolutionary music, adrift but not aimless; in mere months, a jelly buds into being, explosively grows, spews eggs or sperm, and dies, all in cycle with the sun.

The jellyfish becomes a Rorschach test of human reaction.

"Yucky!" one schoolchild yells at their tank at the Seattle Aquarium.

"Pretty!" another exclaims.

"They look like clouds!"

"They look like snow!"

"They look like monsters!"

Here is a creature with which to contemplate what life is, or isn't. Almost all animals in the Northwest move, feed, and reproduce, of course, but the jellies underline what an astounding array of body plans they use to do so.

How to explain to a Martian both the goat and the worm, the seagull and the whelk, the chipmunk and the octopus? How could natural selection account for such variety?

Simply put, every surviving species has a successful strategy—every niche in the environment implies tradeoffs. Witness the frenzy of the fragile hummingbird and the gliding power of the eagle, the agility of the rabbit and the power of the bear, the patience of the reptile and the industry of the beaver.

Animal bodies are lessons in physics. The spindly legs of the sturdy ant would snap if the insect were blown up to elephant size. The pounding heart of a tiny, thin-fleshed mouse would roast an animal with the bulk of a deer. A bird sacrifices sturdiness so it can soar. Clams trade mobility for armor. Form follows function.

Of all the animals, then, which is the most elegant? Which combines great beauty with utter simplicity, languid efficiency with minimal effort, delicacy with venom?

The jellyfish! It is a hallucination, a ghost, a wedding dress, a blowing curtain, an acid trip: one of the most common, ancestral, overlooked, and lovely animals of our inland sea. It can fill the water like a division of paratroopers, glitter with bioluminescence like a chandelier, or undulate like an exotic dancer. It pumps its way through Puget Sound and the San Juan Islands like the beat of an ancient heart.

Small wonder that one-time art student Claudia Mills was drawn to the jellyfish while studying at the University of

Washington's Friday Harbor Laboratories on San Juan Island. After more than twenty years of research, Mills is one of the world's experts on a life form whose importance and ecological role is still barely understood. "It was the visual appeal," she confesses. "They're just really cool looking."

Most of us are animal snobs. We like creatures like ourselves, which means the ones with backbones: mammals, birds, fish, reptiles, and amphibians. Yet 95 percent of the planet's animals do just fine without a backbone, and jellyfish are among the most basic of these.

A jellyfish has no brain, no lungs or gills, no heart, and no bones. It has a gossamer bell to pump it through the water, stinging tentacles to collect food, a stomach, a few nerves to twitch the bell into pulsing, a handful of canals to deliver nutrients, and gonads to make eggs and sperm. That's it. Some jellyfish can sense light, but they have no eyes, nose, ears, or

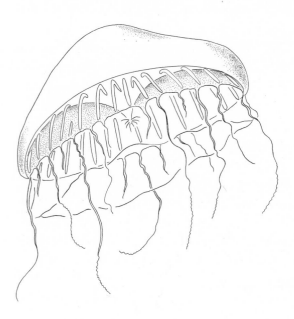

tongue. You can't strip an animal down much more. While humans are 70 percent water, jellyfish are up to 98 percent. There's hardly any there, there.

Much of a jellyfish is truly jelly, a gelatinous goo that isn't even made of living cells. This gluey jelly is trapped between two cell layers: the outside "skin" and the inside lining of muscle that contracts the bell to provide jet propulsion. Between is bulk that isn't even "alive" in the conventional sense of the term. Yet this simplicity has great advantages. Since they are mostly water, it takes very few chemicals, such as carbon, to make a jellyfish. Accordingly, they grow quite rapidly on little food. They are so like their environment that they float with little swimming effort. Their watery mass means they make miserably poor food for predators, a "defense" that has served them well for nearly half a billion years. There's so little to them that their metabolism is slow, meaning they can drift for long periods without eating. They're so simple that some jellyfish can re-grow parts bitten off by enemies.

In other words, less is more.

Jellyfish act like living drift nets, their bell and tentacles catching prey from a large area relative to their size. With no lungs or gills, they draw oxygen through their skin. Many are so transparent they are almost invisible, giving them the ultimate camouflage. Most are tiny, but a few have been recorded with diameters of eight feet or more. Tropical varieties sometimes grow tentacles in excess of thirty feet in length. One, found washed ashore in the Arctic, had a seal's skeleton in its stomach.

Their origin is obscure because jellyfish fossils are understandably quite rare, lacking bone or shell. They are believed to date at least as far back as the Cambrian explosion, that tumultuous evolutionary period 530 million years ago when

complex animals first arose. If so, they far predate the dinosaurs, and this make biological sense. If you wanted to begin
animal evolution with its simplest forms, jellyfish qualify for
the starting lineup. Only sponges and corals are simpler.

It is because of this very simplicity that they remain astonishingly successful. Like many marine species, jellyfish are
seasonal, appearing in spring and dying off in fall. Most aren't
noticed until late summer, when the biggest grow to plate
size, bobbing past a boat or ferry like a floating fried egg.
Yet when Claudia Mills kneels at her Friday Harbor dock in
spring, the water that first appears empty is shown to be filled
with the gossamer parachutes of jellyfish no bigger than a quarter, feeding on tiny, shrimplike copepods that look like floating dust.

Our inland sea blooms with the returning sun like a field
of wildflowers, and each spring uncounted billions of jellyfish
bud into life to eat and be eaten in staggering quantities. What
does this cycle of delicate goo mean to the marine ecosystem
we're spending a small fortune to protect? We haven't a clue.
We know that pollack, the most important commercial fish
in the North Pacific, hides among jellyfish tentacles when
young to avoid other predators. We also know that some
jellyfish are capable of paralyzing and consuming very young
pollack. We know that jellyfish are the occasional prey of fish.
But is jellyfish presence good or bad, from the global and
human point of view? We don't know.

One of the wonderful things about jellyfish is that their
beauty, like that of flowers, is linked to their reproduction.
As they grow like translucent balloons, keeping time to their
own inner music, they are preparing for sex. "The adult
jellyfish is really just a dispersal agent for egg and sperm," Mills
explains. The adults come together in squadrons or schools,

some male and some female, and deposit their DNA in the water for days in a row. Tide and current determine if the two unite and begin forming a small ball of cells. This ball then settles to the bottom or a hard surface and forms what is called a *polyp*, a tiny stalklike creature that represents a jellyfish's winter cycle. It resembles a tiny sea anemone, its near cousin. Some polyps have hard surfaces and others are soft. Some form colonies, with the tubes linking to help feed one another. Some root alone.

The hairy growth on boat hulls is in part composed of jellyfish polyps. Each "hair" will bud a microscopic jellyfish in the spring that breaks off and floats away, growing as it eats plankton in the water. After reaching maximum size, the jellyfish engenders another release of egg and sperm and the cycle starts all over again. Species of jellyfish succeed one another in our waters like a cycle of flowers.

In the deep ocean, where the bottom is impossibly dark and distant, polyps can grow on floating clumps of algae, on swimming snails, or on the skin of fish. Jellyfish are among the most adaptable of animals, ranging from shallows to the abyss. Some jellies spend their lives on the surface. Others swim thousands of feet deep. Many cycle up and down with the rise and fall of the sun. Once started, polyp colonies in shallow water can persist for years, budding each spring. This connection of polyp to pulsing bell is not apparent, and adult jellyfish are so unlike their polyp stage that many were orig-inally classified as separate species. Only now are biologists beginning to link each jellyfish species with its distinctive polyp.

As beautiful as jellyfish are, they can also be scary. Their slow undulation is as ominous as it is mesmerizing. Some trop-ical box jellyfish species, like the sea nettle or the Portuguese man-of-war, can deliver a sting powerful enough to kill or seriously injure a human. Even a few Puget Sound species can sting quite painfully. Tentacles often contain tiny wicked-looking barbs that can fire toxins into the skin of whatever they contact. The poisons can cause pain, swelling, burning, redness, even paralysis, and their scientific names reflect this. One common subclass of jellyfish is called Hydromedusae, for the snake-haired Medusa of Greek mythology.

Still, many local jellyfish don't sting at all, and no Northwest species is lethal to humans. Most jellyfish tentacles are designed to capture small prey such as plankton and fish larvae, not galumphing whales or people. A Hollywood producer once called Mills to ask if it were plausible that a flotilla of jellyfish might attack and kill a diver. When she explained that if was not, he thanked her and put it into a movie anyway.

Gelatinous animals are not easily generalized. The design is so successful that they extend beyond what we call *jellyfish* and fall into at least four separate animal phyla: Cnidaria (which includes jellyfish, coral, and sea anemones); Ctenophora (similar to jellyfish but with a globelike, instead of bell-like, body); Mollusca (swimming, jellylike, plankton-size snails without shell or foot, some of which flap "wings" and are called sea butterflies); and Chordata (which include sea squirts, cylindrical salps, and tadpole-like plankton grazers, all with a primitive nerve cord). We humans are also in the Chordata phylum. It's a little embarrassing that a sea squirt is a distant relative, but that's evolution for you.

As many as half the species in the upper ocean are believed capable of producing their own light through a chemical reaction called *bioluminescence*, similar to that used by fireflies to attract mates. Many jellyfish are among them, some with a string of lights around their rim like the landing lights on a flying saucer.

One common Washington jellyfish species, *Aequorea aequorea*, was once harvested in Friday Harbor, dried, and then shaken to capture its bioluminescent protein. Children were paid a penny each to scoop up the jellies for use in medical research, and a hundred thousand *Aequorea* were harvested per year. Synthetic manufacture of the protein has since eliminated the market. Nor is there a large local market for human consumption, although, jellyfish are eaten in some Asian restaurants. Mills has tried it and doesn't recommend the dish. "It's pretty flavorless."

Other common Washington jellyfish include the clear *Aurelia*, or moon jelly; the large and fringed *Cyanea*, or lion's mane, which stings; and the red- or yellow-bellied *Phacellophora*, or fried egg, which is quite common in southern Puget Sound. Some of the state's most common jellyfish today are believed to be recent invaders, brought here in ship ballast water.

Jellyfish are fussy eaters. Some species prey almost exclusively on other jellyfish, and so ferocious is this jelly-eat-jelly cycle that one researcher has drawn up a food web he calls a "jelly web." Others eat barnacle and clam larvae, copepods, the eggs of other marine invertebrates, other animal plankton, and so on.

Their ecological importance is unclear. In Chesapeake Bay there has been a population explosion of stinging jellyfish since oysters were overharvested. The theory is that with fewer oysters eating plankton, jellies are dining on the surplus bloom. In San Francisco Bay an invasion of a new fingernail-size clam has wiped out the plankton bloom, and the jellyfish population has declined as a result. There's been a tenfold increase in jellyfish in the Bering Sea during the 1990s, an indication of overfishing. "As fisheries get disturbed," Mills explains, "we're ending up with more jellyfish." Just why is not always clear.

Some jellyfish sit on the bottom most of the time, drifting upward only at night. Others feed on the surface. Some have chambers and can float while others will slowly sink if they don't swim. Some flip upside down to feed. One jellyfish the size of a quarter has tentacles six feet long. They have adapted to almost every temperature and every depth. Because the ocean is deep as well as broad—it contains 97 percent of our planet's living space—jellyfish may be one of the planet's most common animals.

It is fascinating that adult jellyfish, which live for only weeks or months, still seem so leisurely as they drift and dream. They have the equanimity of long-term survivors. Could they observe and think, how frantic we humans would seem by comparison! How fast paced! How industrious! Yet all our nets, boats, studies, and speculations are but a blink of time to the jellies. They've survived crashing comets, mass extinctions, global warming, Ice Ages, and the drift of continents. As long as the oceans persist, the jellyfish will persist as well.

The jellyfish is the ultimate tortoise to our hare. Their silent, persistent languor is a message in itself. "We've seen it all," they beat. "Pause, and admire our grace."

Alder

exactly which organism ? see p¹g ²⁷ fixes the nitrogen ;
the actinomycete

SOMETIMES LIFE'S MOST USEFUL THINGS are the most taken for granted, and surely the alder tree is a prime example. Its wood is pulped to make fine paper, but the tree itself has received little ink. It's the most abundant, and most overlooked leafy tree west of the Cascade Mountains. No tree has been so long scorned or has enjoyed such recent rehabilitation. The timber industry has now switched from poisoning alder to planting it. Scientists now sing its praises. Alder is our Cinderella tree.

Just a couple of decades ago, alder was the tree no one would take to the ball. Its flaws are legion. It has no pretty blossoms in the spring and no dramatic color in the fall; its leaves drop green. Its groves are dense, its trunk is as thin and gawky as a teenager, its plain bark relies on lichen to provide an imitation of prettier birch, its wood is soft, and its grain is pale. Alder grows fast, dies quick, and rots quicker.

Foresters used to hate it. Alder invaded clearcuts, shading and killing planted conifer trees such as Douglas fir. Millions of acres of industrial forestland were sprayed with herbicides to get rid of the tree. An alder hillside became a sign of human failure, both to commerce and the environment. No gardener chose alder for a front yard. It was a firewood tree. "The weed of the Northwest," as described by sculptor Duane Pasco, who now carves alder wood into exquisite Native-style masks. Even with alder today selling for nearly as much as fir, alder furniture has been sometimes generically and evasively labeled "hardwood" to avoid being snubbed. Alder was the tree that dared not speak its name.

Then scientists, artisans, and industrialists looked closer. Alder, it turns out, is a beautiful tree ecologically, so perfectly suited to western Washington and Oregon that it fits like a slim foot in a glass slipper. Alder isn't the bane of forestry. It's forestry's salvation. It also turns out to be worth a lot of money. Today, a single good alder saw log can be worth in excess of a hundred dollars. That's some firewood.

If you're not sure which tree is an alder, put on a blindfold and walk into the woods. The first big leaf tree you bump into will probably be one. There are millions in the Pacific Northwest, far more than maple or cottonwood or madrona. Oval leaves with sawtooth edges, pale bark mottled with moss and lichen: that's the one.

Archeological studies of pollen show there is more alder today than at any time since huge forest fires ravaged the region a thousand years ago. This was the tree that invaded the clearcuts where loggers once didn't bother to replant. It colonized decaying roads, abandoned fields, vacant lots, and flooded river bottoms. The tree owes part of its success to its fecundity. A single pound of alder seed can grow more than six hundred thousand new trees. A single tree has been estimated to contain up to 5.4 million seeds. Most fall within a hundred yards, but some can blow for miles. Alder dominated western Washington after the retreat of the Ice Age glaciers, and today it is reclaiming parts of the devastated

ash pan of Mount St. Helens. It loves wounded soil. It is our healer.

There are thirty species of alder in the world, but the principal one in the Pacific Northwest is the red alder. This is the biggest of the American varieties, reaching heights of up to one hundred feet. A record holder near Astoria, Oregon, has a trunk twenty feet in circumference.

Red alder's name begins to hint at its subtle charm. It blushes a brownish-red in the early spring when its male catkins—"flower" tassels dangling like thousands of phalluses on each tree to fertilize the smaller female cones—burst with pollen in riotous, rust-colored sexuality. Alder-covered hillsides flush like a pale Valentine card. It's an erotic tree.

It also bleeds red when cut, its wood darkening from white to brown, and the red rind under its bark is so intense that Indians used it for paint. They also steeped its bark in water to treat rheumatic fever. Scientists later discovered that the bark contains salicin, an ingredient in modern medicines.

Alder's ecological role has been fully appreciated only in recent years. Not only does the tree prolifically re-seed burned, cut, or ravaged sites, it also fertilizes them. It eliminates soil diseases that prey on conifer species. Then it effectively starves itself to make way for a new crop of fir, hemlock, or cedar. All this for free.

The fact that it takes a human lifespan for this cycle to take place leaves some of us impatient with alder. We like our fertilizer to come by the bag. But at least nine major timber companies in Washington and Oregon have switched from relentlessly eradicating alder (though some of that still goes on) to planting it. "We know alder benefits the soil," said Del Fisher, a Weyerhaeuser lands manager who has overseen the planting of several thousand acres of alder by the company in recent years. "Just how *much* benefit is still being researched."

The Indians knew alder was a useful soft "hardwood" (lumber lingo for leafy deciduous trees) long before the pioneers showed up. They used it for cooking utensils because it was easy to carve and, unlike cedar, imparted no flavor to the food and didn't splinter in the mouth. They shaped it with obsidian, bone, and beaver teeth.

Loggers were more scornful. Given the initial supply of huge old-growth fir, hemlock, and cedar, why bother with alder? It was pathetically slender compared with the evergreen giants. The tree was so weak it couldn't hold up its own weight after eighty years or so, tending to fall over ignominiously. The wood was spongy and decayed quickly. It was relatively worthless as structural timber.

Then came the end of the old-growth supply along with a growing public demand for blond-wood furniture—and an industry that had millions of "firewood trees" on its lands.

Beginning in the 1980s, big timber companies decided it might be more cost-effective to sell alder than to kill it. They began pushing it as a stylish hardwood in Europe and Asia. Foreigners, free of our prejudices, gave it a try and agreed. The wood was light, blond, and worked and finished well. Sales took off. During the peak of the battle over the spotted owl, alder harvests jumped nearly 30 percent in compensation for the decline in conifer harvests.

Acre for acre, say Weyerhaeuser executives, fast-growing alder can make as much money for a timber company as fir or hemlock. It grows faster, has few knots, and the wood color is consistent from heart to edge. Because it competes with other fast-growing species for light, alder grows densely for a leaf tree, with optimum tree-farm spacing of about six hundred trees per acre. Oak and maple demand a lot more elbow room. "Its form is optimal for a broadleaf tree seeking to grow in dense competition," notes Reinhard Stettler, a forest genetics expert at the University of Washington in Seattle. "There is very little you can improve on it geometrically." The result is that a grower can pack a lot of wood to the acre. Go to a new alder stand in a disturbed area such as Mount St. Helens and you can barely penetrate it. Branches have sprouted to absorb almost every square inch of falling sunlight, crowding any competitor out. The space within seems jammed with fast-growing wood. Like a squirming fifth grader, alder is a tree that pushes to the head of the line.

Ecology, however, is what really makes this once dowdy species glow. Alder is the species that fertilizes forest soil in much the same way that alfalfa fertilizes crop soils. Both take nitrogen out of the air and "fix" it into the ground, where plants can use it. This amending of cut and ravaged landscapes takes place underground. Alder roots form a three-way part-

nership with a moldlike bacterial organism called Actinomycete, and a mycorrhizal fungus.

The actinomycetal mold grows on the alder roots. There-
upon the alder delivers nutrients to the mold, which in turn
chemically converts nitrogen from the atmosphere into a form
that the alder and other plants can use as food. In other words,
mold and tree feed each other, a trick that conifer trees such
as Douglas fir can't match. That means the alder can colonize barren soils where other trees would starve. Later, rotting alder leaves and logs deposit this new nitrogen into the
soil at a rate of up to a thousand pounds per acre.

Meanwhile, the mycorrhizal fungus improves the efficiency of alder roots. Mycorrhizae first gained fifteen minutes
of fame during the spotted owl battle because the dispersal
of the fungus depends in part on small mammals that live in
old-growth forests. No old growth, no rodents. No rodents,
no rodent droppings that redistribute the fungus spores. And
without fungi, none of the healthy soil for the giant trees that
make old growth in the first place. We annihilate our ecosystem at future peril. The fungus remains important to Northwest trees because it expands their root surface area, helping
each tree extract nutrients and water from a volume of soil
hundreds of times larger than it could unaided. In return, the
tree feeds the fungus with carbon and vitamins.

The three organisms together are greater than the sum of
their parts. The mold actually promotes the growth of the fungus, and both spur the growth of alder, which can reach the
height of a three-storey building in as little as five years. Alder
is at full height in just forty years, rapidly reforesting barren
ground. The elegance of the partnership does not end there,
however. The soil organisms accelerate alder's absorption of
phosphorus from the soil, a draining so complete that a new

stand of alder can't succeed its parents on the same ground. University of Washington soils scientist Dale Cole notes the significance for forest health. The alder, having worked so hard to improve the soil, politely gets out of the way by dying off and making room for conifers. The evergreen trees don't need the missing phosphorus but crave the added nitrogen. Because of alder, their growth is enhanced: studies show that stands of mixed fir and alder grow at twice the rate of a neighboring grove of fir alone. "It's a marriage made in heaven," says Cole.

A generation of alder also poisons laminated root rot, a soil disease that can ravage Douglas fir. The rot dies back sufficiently so that a new crop of conifers can grow on a once-infected site, keeping the disease in check. In sum, foresters learned they were poisoning a tree that was working as both natural fertilizer and vaccination. Alder was there for a reason.

Alder groves also play host to nearly two hundred animal species that use the thickets to reproduce in, and another two hundred species that use them to feed. If that's not enough, alder's wet, spongy nature also makes it resistant to forest fires. It not only reseeds burned forests but it serves as a natural firebreak to keep future fires at a smaller size. These discoveries are more like rediscoveries of long-observed experience. English poet William Browne gave tribute in verse to the tree, which also grows in Britain, as long ago as 1613: "The alder, whose fat shadow nourish, each plant set near him (will) long flourish."

Alas, few modern poems are written to alder. It's never going to have the beauty of Japanese cherry or quaking aspen, never the majesty of redwood and fir, never the noble umbrella of oak and elm. Its looks have the anonymity that experts say makes a good spy.

Still, a mature grove of ghostly slanting trunks and dappled green light has a subtle lineal beauty. The pale bark is marvelously patterned by the darker lichen and moss that use it as a host, giving the grove a look reminiscent of columns of marble. Its thick canopy casts a green shade as deep and mysterious as a vast aquarium. Certainly stands of alder relieve the grand monotony of conifer woods. They're a splash of springtime lime, a haunting rustle at the threat of a mountain thunderstorm, a tracery of black branch against our gun-gray winter skies.

And it's not bad firewood. Splits easily, burns cleanly, makes coals fast.

There's a lesson in all this. Alder didn't change over the last few decades, we did. The tree went in our perception from pest to product, an evolving attitude that should give us pause in our tendency to play favorites with species. In retrospect, the aerial spraying of herbicides to annihilate alder seems not just wrong, but arrogantly so.

Alder seems put in place to serve many purposes. One of these may be to humble our quick judgments, reminding us of our own place in the scheme of things.

Deer

*male German Shepherd's
care of fawns*

W E S E E T H E M M O S T F R E Q U E N T L Y A T
dawn and dusk, an apparition from the wild that
never fails to give reassurance. Deer dash across our roads,
mince shyly into our yards, or browse the edges of meadows
like a reminder of Northwest magic. They have a dancer's
step. At night they run in dreams of myth and history. They
are mankind's most dependably enduring symbol of the
wild.

Deer were painted on cave walls as ochre figures of power
and grace. Diana, goddess of the hunt, had a stag as companion. Robin Hood poached the King's deer. American
writer James Fenimore Cooper invented the Deerslayer as a
symbol of frontier prowess. Daniel Boone and Davy Crockett
made fiction into fact. Antlers once were a standard decora-
tion of lodges and rural restaurants. *Bambi* was a child's introduction to nature, and *The Yearling* taught us about growing
up. For generations, hunting was a boy's rite of passage. *The
Deer Hunter* contrasted the ritual of the hunt with the horror of Vietnam.

Deer fed the American frontier. They were as important
to eastern Indians and early white pioneers as buffalo were

to the Great Plains or salmon to the Northwest. The animal supplied not just meat but hide for clothing, bone and antlers for tools, sinew for thread, and hooves for glue and rattles. So abundant were deer that their skins became a colonial export. In one eighteen-year period, hides from six hundred thousand deer were shipped from Savannah, Georgia, to England.

By the end of the nineteenth century, deer were near extinction east of the Mississippi and in serious decline in the West. Since then, hunting regulations and the animal's adaptability has produced a comeback. Deer forage on the browse created by clearcut logging, the food of farms and gardens, and the water and crops of irrigation districts. Today, there may be as many as twenty million deer in the United States, including four hundred thousand in Washington State alone. They are the most common large mammal of the wild; curious, beautiful, furtive, and shy.

They might also seem, at first glance, so familiar as to be boring. There are nearly as many deer in Washington State as there are people within the city limits of Seattle. Their routine plant browsing offers little everyday drama. Deer, after all, are ruminants, or cud chewers: cows with grace, the cynic could contend. Like cows, they are walking compost piles. Their four-chambered stomach uses bacteria to progressively break down vegetation so it can be decomposed. Deer usually browse shrubs and trees instead of grasses because their digestive enzymes have evolved to process that kind of forest feed. They chew and digest, chew and digest.

One look tells us that deer differ from a dull domestic, however. These animals are intelligent and agile, and their senses of smell and hearing are excellent. The big ear on an adult mule deer has a reflective surface of forty-two square inches, like a living satellite dish. The round, protruding eyes give them a 310–degree range of view and excellent night vision. Deer may be color-blind, but they are difficult to sneak up on. In fact, they regularly outwit us.

"Washington still has the highest density of hunters per square mile of any western state," says Rolf Johnson, director of the deer and elk program of the state's Department of Fish and Wildlife. There have been about one hundred and seventy thousand deer hunters in recent years, down from a peak of about three hundred thousand back in the early 1970s but still a huge army to sweep our woods. Yet despite such numbers of both hunters and deer, only one in five of the human stalkers are typically successful. Deer see many more hunters than hunters see deer. They sit so still that a human can walk right by them, and they are so crafty that they sometimes follow a hunter to keep an eye on him.

Similarly, deer regularly defy the best efforts of researchers and cause millions of dollars of damage by nibbling on seedlings, food crops, and gardens. Dale Nolte, field station leader of the National Wildlife Research Center in Olympia, has seen entire seedling plantings wiped out by herds of migrating deer. Timber companies have tried to scare them away by firing loud propane cannons, or by festooning branches with tinsel strips of Mylar, or enshrouding the trees with yellow mesh, or topping seedlings with plastic cones, or spraying them with synthetic urine from wolves and coyotes. Nothing works permanently. Eventually, deer get wise to all the tricks.

These ruminants are superb athletes. They can sustain speeds up to thirty-five miles per hour, leap up to thirty feet horizontally, and jump barriers as high as eight feet. They are excellent swimmers, with the does sometimes swimming to small islands in the San Juans to give birth undisturbed.

Columbia whitetail deer have been observed swimming several miles off the Northwest coast, and one deer in Alaska was seen swimming fourteen miles from one island to another. They've been clocked at a steady water pace of ten miles per hour, or faster than most sailboats.

They are also one of the most adaptive of all animals, with relatives found almost everywhere on the planet but Antarctica and the worst of the Sahara desert. There are more than forty species, and one hundred and ninety subspecies, of deer throughout the world.

Washington and Oregon have four distinct regional populations. Blacktail deer, a forest-adapted subspecies of the West's dominating mule deer, are the primary inhabitant west of the Cascades. They are the most likely to be spotted by residents of the Puget Sound basin and Willamette Valley.

There is also a small, endangered population of six hundred Columbia whitetail deer centered around the Julia Butler Hansen National Wildlife Refuge near Cathlamet, on the Columbia River. Pushed near extinction by diking and development of the Willamette and lower Columbia valleys, these deer remain at a precarious level because of periodic flooding of their refuge and coyote predation.

East of the Cascades the state is dominated by the mule deer, the most common deer of the West and identified by its large, mule-like ears. Mule deer are losing ground, however, because their strategy of sprinting from danger and then stopping—a tactic that worked in the bow and arrow days— dooms them to a high-powered rifle with scope. "They're suckers for long-range weapons," remarks Jack Nelson, a retired deer specialist from Washington State University.

Civilization has its benefits, however. Irrigation has opened new range for Northwest mule deer. Farms have proven even more beneficial to the eastern whitetail deer that dominate the eastern United States and are now spreading across the Columbia Basin. The wily whitetail has followed agriculture westward and someday might reach Cathlamet's isolated whitetail population and interbreed. Blacktails and mule deer will also interbreed. Telling these deer apart is difficult for a nonexpert since all have a mixture of white and black on their tails, an appendage that helps them recognize their own kind and serves as a white flag when raised to signal danger or lust.

Deer tend to be bigger in our imaginations than in reality. At their shoulder, mature westside animals usually aren't much more than waist-high to an adult human. At one and a half years, Washington's blacktail deer average around one hundred pounds, while in five and a half years, a buck will reach two hundred pounds and a doe about one hundred and thirty. If harvested, about 40 percent of this total weight is edible meat.

While few bucks survive more than a couple of years because of hunting, a healthy deer can live to ten years or more in the wild, and in excess of twenty years in captivity. They pack enormous change into each year of this lifespan, their bodies locked to a sexual cycle timed to the annual shift in the hours of sunlight that signal how much plant food will be available. Deer mate in the fall after fattening all summer, with well-fed does able to conceive in their first year of life. Fertilization usually produces twins or triplets in the womb, but a pregnant female may reabsorb one or more of the fetuses if the winter is too hard and there is not food enough to sustain her and her young.

Birth occurs about six and a half months after conception, in the spring, and newborn deer develop rapidly to survive.

The fawns average from six to eight pounds at birth and begin nursing and standing within minutes. Even as they do so, the mother eats her afterbirth to regain some of the nutrients her pregnancy has cost her, and she licks her newborn clean. Her milk has twice the butterfat of a cow's, and a fawn will double its size in a week. In six months, its weight will have increased tenfold.

One way that mothers keep track of their wandering young is through the trail of scent left by a gland at the base of the hooves. Deer use smell for a variety of cues, and adult bucks will sometimes stamp the ground to leave an odor that warns rivals and attracts does. Both sexes also deliberately urinate on a tuft of hair at the midpoint of their rear legs; they identify each other by sniffing this untidy but eminently practical calling card.

As spring advances, some deer will migrate slowly back to higher elevations, eating as they go. While females remain preoccupied with their young, sunlight is triggering sexual change in males.

Bucks grow and shed a set of antlers each year, starting in spring. While horns are made of material similar to human fingernails, antlers are true bone, though without marrow inside. Their growth begins when sunlight absorbed through the eye stimulates the deer's pituitary gland, triggering a growth hormone.

Antlers can grow as fast as half an inch a day and have so much blood beneath the covering velvet, delivering calcium for growth, that they are hot to the touch when lengthening. The rack is tender during the four months it takes to grow. The common belief that a buck's age can be told by the number of points on its antlers is true to a rough extent but untrue as an exact measure. Nutrition and heredity are as important as age in establishing the size of the rack.

As autumn nears and sunlight wanes, the pituitary gland shuts off antler growth and another hormone triggers the growth of the male's testicles. The antlers harden, their surrounding velvet dries and is rubbed off, and rising levels of testosterone enlarge blood vessels in the neck, causing it to swell. The buck begins to look like a football lineman, ready to butt head over mates.

While fights occur during the fall mating season to establish territory, combat is dangerous and thus infrequent; one purpose of elaborate antlers is to warn off smaller male rivals without a struggle. The mating itself helps exhaust the buck's supply of testosterone, triggering the antlers to fall off painlessly at the beginning of winter. On the forest floor, they become a source of calcium nibbled at by many creatures, including the deer themselves.

During the rutting season, bucks follow does to wait for their female estrus period, which will last only about twenty-four hours in each twenty-eight-day lunar cycle. When estrus happens, does will mate several times in a day if possible and then ward off bucks when pregnancy occurs. Bucks expend so much energy and eat so little during this period that they can lose a quarter to a third of their body weight. After their antlers fall off, they eat voraciously to get ready for winter.

In summer, deer can be plagued by ticks, fleas, flies, and worms, but winter is their most dangerous time. Because unchecked deer herds can increase at rates of 50 to 100 percent per year until famine or disease intervenes, wildlife managers contend that it is not a question of whether deer will necessarily be thinned, but how. In areas where hunting was banned and predators were eliminated, deer numbers exploded so fast that shrubs were eaten bare. The deer populations completely collapsed.

Reasoning that a bullet or arrow is more merciful than starvation, officials set the hunting season each fall to keep deer in balance with their environment. Counting deer is difficult, and predicting the severity of the coming winter is impossible, so game management is as much art as science. Officials have succeeded, however, in keeping deer numbers in rough equilibrium.

Hunting is not the only source of deer mortality. Animal predators such as cougar, coyote, and dogs also take a high toll, and automobiles kill more deer each year in the United States than do hunters. Lisa Shipley, a professor of wildlife biology at Washington State University, has noted that certain sections of roadway in her state average twenty deer killed per kilometer per year. Highway departments across the country have experimented with fences, mirrors that reflect headlights back into the woods, or artificial wolf urine to frighten deer away from roads by smell.

As species, Northwest deer are in no danger. A survivor of the Ice Ages, they are one of the most adaptable of woodland creatures, thriving around farmland, clearcuts, suburbs, and tree farms. They devour rose bushes and will eat so many apples that they bloat. Individually, however, they live a life on edge, ready to bolt at the first sign of danger and struggling with parasites, predators, cold, and hunger. While there are more deer in the Pacific Northwest today than when pioneers arrived—because logging, gardening, and agriculture have created more feed—the total population is believed to be declining as houses gobble up forest habitat.

What is enchanting about deer, however, is how gracefully they integrate with their environment. Elusive one day, boldly browsing the next, they materialize and vanish like the seasons, with a spring contentment or an autumn exaltation we can envy. It was Samuel Butler who commented: "All animals except man know that the ultimate of life is to enjoy it." Deer, we suspect, are proof of this maxim. Surely their enduring presence helps us enjoy life as well.

Gulls

no gulls fouled by oil spill in SF Bay

R ICHARD BACH'S ROMANCE WITH FLIGHT began in boyhood when he watched gulls glide the updraft along the breakwater of California's Corona del Mar. They swooped, rolled, and soared, suspended on air "without strings or wire."

"You could hear the sound of their passing," the Stanwood, Washington, author recalls. "You could hear the wind on their wings. Here, it seemed, was the perfect creature: the one with all the attributes my soul yearned to own."

Bach famously did take to the air, first as a pilot. Then, after flying Air Force fighters, he got an idea for a spiritual allegory based on gulls. "It was a story that struck me as something already finished," he recalls. This proved too optimistic. He hurriedly wrote two-thirds of a short book, stalled, and then eight years later woke from a vivid dream and completed the manuscript.

The rest is publishing legend. Every publisher in New York turned down the "talking seagull book." Then an editor at Macmillan who had liked Bach's two earlier books on human flight asked him if he had anything else lying around, unaware her bosses had already passed on a bird named Jonathan. He sent it once more, she secured a modest first printing of five thousand copies, and in 1970 lightning struck.

The little gull that could was a perfect hero for a troubled time. *Jonathan Livingston Seagull* sold more than thirty million copies in forty languages. In its wake, Bach made and lost a fortune, dissolved one marriage and found another, made up with an estranged son, and wrote a series of books as cherished by some readers for their insights as they are scorned by others for their sentiment. The magic of *Jonathan* was not just its writing, but how it captured the glories of gulls in flight.

Bach is no ornithologist and only the most casual of bird watchers. He cheerfully admits he did little biological research for his phenomenal book. Yet for millions of people he captured the spirit of one of the most lovely, amusing, cheeky, obnoxious, and commonly observed of all wild animals. There's something about gulls, and Bach managed to turn a garbage dump bird into a link with God.

Dennis Paulson, director of the Slater Museum of Natural History at the University of Puget Sound and a gull expert, remembers reading *Jonathan* with familiar pleasure. The birds have fascinated him as they did Bach. The ornithologist has just one niggling criticism, for which no layman can really be blamed. Scientifically, Paulson points out, there is no such thing as a seagull.

Gulls, yes—half a dozen species frequent our Northwest and as many more casually visit—but scientists don't attach the appellation "sea" to any of them. Ring-billed gulls nest at Potholes Reservoir near Moses Lake. Bonaparte's gulls breed in Alaskan and Canadian lakes. Heermann's gulls migrate from the Gulf of California to British Columbia. Gulls fly

the Columbia River, make nests in old-growth forest, and shuttle across Snoqualmie Pass. A lot of "seagulls" never see an ocean.

The Mormons have built a Salt Lake City monument to California gulls because they devoured a plague of locusts in 1848. "I heard the voice of fowl flying overhead and saw a flock of seven gulls," one pioneer reported. "They came faster and more of them until the heavens were darkened." It seemed a visitation miracle, and perhaps it was.

But California gulls nest in the tens of thousands by the Great Salt Lake, and the pioneers' growing cloud of gulls exhibited classic feeding behavior: gulls routinely follow their fellows who seem to be finding food. One reason the bird is white is so that it can be spotted by its kind from great distances when clustering to feed, drawing more and more in like gravity. Gulls are a "me-too" bird.

Still, the saving of the early Utah settlement is representative of what has become a close human-bird relationship. We feed them and they clean up after us. Gull numbers in the Pacific Northwest have exploded ten times or more since European settlement, Paulson estimates. They are litter pickers, scavengers, and thieves, thriving on our discards, cannery offal, and the field worms turned up by tractors or wiggling to the surface of golf courses and playing fields after a heavy rain. "I call them klepto-parasites," he says. "These birds evolved on wild, remote coasts. To see one on a dumpster in the morning is a reminder how much our world has changed." They are also feisty, greedy bullies, gobbling the eggs and chicks of puffins and terns, and stealing fish from a pelican's pouch or an otter's chest.

Gulls must be forgiven their bad manners, of course, because they're so beautiful when they play in high winds, using their pointed wings like a kite. Biologists have no idea if animals with a brain the size of a gull's have any sense of play, but certainly they convey a kind of joy. Their cry is haunting. The sun sometimes shines through their wings as if through an angel's gown, giving them a Jonathan-like ethereal glow.

Gulls are relatively plain for a bird, being mostly white and gray. The reason is practical. Their white bellies make gulls less visible to fish when flying overhead or floating on the water. Scandinavian scientists painted gull bellies dark and noted that their feeding efficiency sharply declined. Gulls also feed best in flocks, where prey escaping one bird might dart into the path of another. Accordingly, their congregations help the individual as well as the group. So instinctual is this bunching that biologists have watched the birds converge on a thrown white handkerchief.

Identification can be difficult, because the differences between gull species are subtle to our eyes. The problem is made worse because all young gulls tend to have brown plumage that takes three to four years to mature to the white of a sexually mature adult. Sievert Rohwer, bird curator at the University of Washington's Burke Museum of Natural History and Culture, suspects the brown plumage—a handicap when feeding at sea—is useful camouflage on the beach. Younger birds scavenge shores for food that older, more experienced gulls have missed. Their dull coloring gives them time to eat before a bullying elder notices and zooms in to rob them.

A rare highlight of color can be found on the adult's bright yellow beak. That peculiar red spot is where their young peck to encourage mom and dad to regurgitate food into their hungry beaks. So instinctual is this behavior that researchers have found that chicks will peck at a red spot on a yellow stick that looks nothing like a gull.

The eastern North Pacific has one of the richest concentrations of seabirds in the world. Alaska is estimated to have forty million seabirds, and Washington's Protection Island alone is home to forty-four thousand. Gulls are in the bird order (Charadriiformes) that includes sandpipers, skuas, murres, auklets, and puffins.

Two varieties of gulls breed here: Glaucous-winged (meaning gray-winged) and western. Many of the gulls seen in our Northwest—the Mew, the California, Bonaparte's, the Ring-billed, Heermann's—are passing through on their way to breeding grounds. In all, thirteen species of gull have been spotted in the Pacific Northwest—nearly a third of the world's total—and October is the time when local gull populations are at or near their migratory peak.

Maybe we like gulls because they seem comfortably average. If Bach's Jonathan represented the everyman trying to achieve a higher plane, gulls in real life are a kind of every-bird. Albatrosses and petrels are superbly designed to soar, but albatrosses have vast wingspans and can't turn tightly. Penguins, though flightless and clumsy, are excellent swimmers. Gulls are an adaptive compromise: shorter and wider than a petrel, they are able flyers, middling swimmers with smaller webbed feet, adequate walkers for the same reason, and modest divers. They are merely okay at twisting to catch popcorn thrown into the air, and while cormorants can dive down to a depth of one hundred feet, gulls seldom do more than poke their heads underwater. Weighing about two to three pounds, gulls are neither dramatically big nor small. They are moderates in physique.

It works.

Gulls are also comfortable with humans, being too oily for us to enjoy as food and officially protected from hunters because of their usefulness as sanitation engineers. They live long enough—one gull on a Rhode Island lightship lived forty-four years—to learn our ways. Gulls are bold around us, and it is no accident that Alfred Hitchcock used gulls and crows, two groups of birds particularly adapted to our presence, as the primary marauders in his classic horror film, *The Birds*.

In the nearly four decades since that film, canneries have closed, ships have curbed their spewing of garbage, and dumps have been replaced with sanitary landfills. Scientists haven't done census studies to determine if gull populations are declining as a result, but if they are, it will predictably relieve stress on other seabird species. Rohwer notes that gull success is a prime example of one of the most overlooked problems in conservation: species overabundance. Animals that adapt well to humans may push other endangered species even closer to the edge. Gulls are a good example. Atlantic puffins were driven to near extinction by the increase of the rival birds.

The Old English word for gull is *mew*, indicative of its cry. "Gull" itself may come from the Breton *gwel-a*, meaning to weep, and certainly the keening call of gulls is one of the most familiar sounds in all nature, as distinctive as the ocean's roar. Their Japanese name translates as "sea cats" for the mewing sound they make.

The most frequently sighted gulls in the Seattle area are probably the Glaucous-winged and, in winter, the smaller but similar looking Mew. The Glaucous-winged gull will nest on buildings, ferry piers, old pilings, and derelict boats, and is resident enough to deserve the term "native."

Gulls will eat almost anything, from apples to sea stars, swallowing an arm or two of the latter and starting to digest the catch in its throat while the rest is still hanging out of its beak. They've been observed eating sea urchins, carrion, young rabbits, and beetles. They regularly crack open shellfish by dropping them from the air onto rocks, and I once had a window hit by a "flying clam" dropped by a gull in a windstorm. Paulson has observed the birds learning this trick: young gulls are initially puzzled when the same tactic doesn't work by dropping clams onto mud. Trial and error gets it right.

Gulls can drink seawater because a gland at the top of their head extracts the salt. If you see liquid dripping from the end of a gull's beak, it is likely the resulting saline solution being secreted.

Although their bodies must be kept a piping one hundred

degrees in internal temperature, gulls are supremely comfortable in the most miserable of Northwest weather. Their feathers keep them dry and warm, and they preen this natural blanket with oil from a gland near the tail. Only their beaks and feet get cold. A gull balancing on one leg is probably warming the other.

Like many birds, gulls are fairly monogamous, mating for life and rejoining each other at breeding time with yodeling cries of recognition. Males woo females in part by regurgitating food into their beaks, a romantic tactic not recommended for a human restaurant date. Most gulls nest in colonies, staking out a nest site in what can be an initial squabble over territory. After mating, females typically lay three eggs. In a pattern followed by some other bird species, males spend slightly more time incubating the eggs than females. Both parents share in the task of feeding the young after hatching.

As with many wild animals, early mortality is high. A British Columbia study showed that up to a third of the eggs failed to hatch, and up to a quarter of the chicks that did emerge didn't survive to fledgling stage. Chicks that leave their own nest run the risk of being cannibalized by other adult gulls. Death is also common the first couple of years, when gulls are less experienced at finding food. Yet if a gull survives this early gauntlet, it winds up crafty and hardy enough to live for decades.

And if "seagull" is technically incorrect, gulls certainly concentrate in tidal areas because of the abundance of food exposed at low tide. Accordingly, the Northwest might credit the presence of its gulls to the pull of the moon. When Rohwer led a collecting expedition to the South Pacific, his students found plenty of terns but no gulls, presumably because of the lack of tidal change at the equator.

So, a bird of moderate speed and endurance, a hanger on, a garbage gourmand, a squawker. Why was Jonathan *this* bird? Why does almost everyone stop once in a while and watch the gull with pleasure?

Somehow gulls fit our landscape and our mindscape. One can no more imagine the Pacific Northwest without gulls than without Mount Rainier, Douglas fir, and the smell of salt wind. We're triggered to respond to animals as we respond to beauty, danger, or remembered scents. Snakes provoke fascinated fear; a hooked salmon, a thrill; slugs, a curious revulsion; and horses, a partnership. Children understand this better than grown-ups do.

Gulls pull their own kind of trigger. They evoke peace. Maybe it's their relationship with water, so soothing in itself. Maybe it's their reliable presence, reassuring us that no matter how rapid our own growth, some connection to the natural world remains. Maybe it's their color, a spot of brightness on the darkest days. And maybe it's the sheer exultation of their flight, a grace and ambition that seems to go beyond the mere need to gather food and reflects the energy of the planet itself.

Richard Bach understood this. Jonathan the seagull was a bird of possibility. Isn't it possibility—the chance of finding a meaningful and joyful life—that has always drawn people to the Pacific Northwest?

Sea Otters

Lootas' babies

YOU'RE HERE BECAUSE OF THE SEA OTTER.
Not here on Earth, but *here*, in the Pacific Northwest.
Long before there were Microsoft or Boeing or Weyerhaeuser
or salmon canneries or gold mines, there was one surpass-
ingly soft, luxuriant, tantalizing, and fabulously rich resource
that brought risk-taking entrepreneurs to what was the most
distant and gloomy of all Euro-American destinations: our
fog-shrouded, rock-studded coast.

Vitus Bering and Captain James Cook came to look for a
Northwest Passage. They sent back reports of a slow, friendly,
buoyant marine mammal with an astonishing half-million
hairs per square inch of skin, or about fifty times more than
today's most thickly maned human shampoo models. The
explorers' predictions of instant wealth brought a stampede
of sea captains. The Chinese would pay the equivalent of one
hundred dollars—big money in the eighteenth century—for
a pelt that Native Americans would trade for scrap metal. A
three-year voyage could produce a 300 percent profit. Economic empires could be founded on fur.

The first sea otters encountered by Russian fur traders were
so tame that they nuzzled the traders' legs—and were quickly

48

bludgeoned to death. The Russians chased otter almost as far south as San Francisco even as the British, Spanish, and Americans sailed north. Bostonian Robert Gray stumbled onto the Columbia River while trading for the pelts.

Aleut Indians were enslaved by traders to harvest the animals. Disease ran rampant, maps were drawn, forts were built. Most people are only dimly aware of sea otters today, and yet at one time they were all the region was known for: they were the Bill Gates, Starbucks, and Amazon.com of the 1700s all rolled into one. The sea otter set in motion a tumultuous transformation of the Pacific Northwest that continues to this day.

The animal also went nearly extinct, declining from an estimated three hundred thousand otters in the North Pacific when the Russians first crossed Siberia, to fewer than two thousand in 1911. Seattle's Karl Kenyon, dean of otter researchers, has estimated half a million were harvested before the fur rush went bare. Washington's sea otter population was wiped out entirely. A "keystone species" of our coastal ecosystem was annihilated to the last animal.

Today, however, there are an estimated 100 to 150 thousand sea otters in the North Pacific, thanks to a hunting ban. In 1970 a group of fifty-nine otters was transplanted from Alaska to Washington's Olympic coast. After decades of edgy survival, the population first stabilized and then began to grow. It now numbers about six hundred and is currently expanding at a rate of 11 percent a year. Their comeback is as astonishing a story as that of the gray whale and the bald eagle.

It is also heartwarming. If you like your animals warm, fuzzy, joyous, and cute, then the sea otter and its frenetic cousin, the river otter—which marine mammal biologist C. J. Casson of the Seattle Aquarium describes as "the sea otter on caffeine"—are for you. They are true Valentine animals:

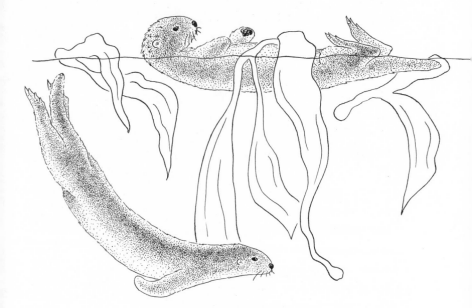

their pelts sensuous, their cavorting like foreplay, their sociability enviable, and their beauty arresting. River otter mating is vigorous, noisy, and lengthy, with copulation lasting up to twenty-five minutes.

Who wouldn't want to be reincarnated as an otter?

And yet when it was announced in Cordova, Alaska, that hundreds of sea otters were dying in the wake of the Exxon Valdez oil spill, the assembled fishermen cheered. Adult otters, the males of which can reach a hundred pounds, must eat a quarter of their body weight per day to stay warm and alive. They like the same shellfish and crabs humans do. On our own coast they are beginning to compete with Makah tribal fisheries for commercial shellfish and with campers for razor clams.

Casson notes that if an adult man ate like a sea otter, he would consume one hundred and eighty quarter-pound hamburger patties each day. It costs the Seattle Aquarium from five to ten thousand dollars a year to feed a typical otter. One of their animals, Lootas, gobbled fifty to one hundred and fifty mussels a day when growing.

Nor is the male sea otter quite the ideal Valentine. He hangs out with the guys until the mood strikes him, bumps and annoys a fertile female until she agrees to submit, and then bites her on the nose to hold her in place while mating. A female's normally black nose can be red and raw for weeks afterward. The male then leaves, having nothing to do with the pups he fathered and choosing a different mate the next time.

We fall for otters anyway. Their faces were invented to enchant. They have the grace of mermaids and the energy of gymnasts. They snooze like furry angels. Gluttons or not, they're as lovable as teddy bears.

Companiable "rafts" of up to one hundred and twenty-five lounging sea otters can be spotted in summer in the kelp beds off Cape Alava on Washington's Olympic coast, says Steve Jeffries, a marine mammal researcher at the state Department of Fish and Wildlife. You'll need good binoculars or a spotting scope to watch them as they wrap themselves in a kelp frond, anchoring themselves in the swell. The animal currently ranges from Destruction Island near Kalaloch to Seiku on the Strait of Juan de Fuca. At one time they extended down the Pacific coast to central California, but biologists doubt that sea otters have ever lived farther east than Port Angeles on the Strait of Juan de Fuca.

Locals who claim to have spotted sea otters in the San Juan Islands have actually spotted their smaller cousin, the river otter, which often bounds down a beach to hunt in salt water. River otters are half the weight of their marine relatives and are easily identified by their long and tapering tail. They can sprint up to eighteen miles per hour on land, and they den on shore. They tend to swim on their bellies whereas sea otters paddle on their backs.

River otters are the playground kids of the animal kingdom. They slide on snow, playfully wrestle, touch muzzles, holler, flip, splash, balance, poke, and make whoopee. Their language is universal. Party on! The slightly more staid sea otters are extremely clumsy on land and spend almost all their time on their backs at sea, the air in their fur keeping them as buoyant as a life jacket. It's life in a cruise chair. They sleep, feed, mate, give birth, and raise their young at sea. If it seems amazing that marine mammals such as whales and dolphins were once land animals that returned to the ocean, an example of such transition can be observed in the progressive water adaptation of river and sea otters.

A good place to see the difference between river and sea otters is the Seattle Aquarium, which has an exhibit of each. There the staff has learned first hand the mischievous ingenuity of otters. One river otter maneuvered a log to make a ladder up the waterfall of the naturalistic exhibit and wound up on the roof of his home before being recaptured. At the city's Woodland Park Zoo, river otters at the modern Northern Trail exhibit can be watched chasing down a regular feeding of live trout with ease, playing with them like a cat before devouring them.

Sea otters match their curiosity with strength. Aquarium otters have managed to lift fifty-pound rocks off the bottom and bang them until chips break off. In California they've been observed using Coke bottles as tools and turning over tin cans on the bottom to find hiding octopuses. At the Seattle Aquarium they have opened unlocked doors, stuffed coins and shells into any available crack, and broken windows. One otter burst free, made a circuit of the marine mammal exhibits while leaving a trail of bloody paw prints, and finding nothing superior to the girls he left behind, returned to his own pool.

Visitors given a peek at poolside must beware. The otters have shredded a necktie, grabbed hats and sunglasses, and almost spilled a television cameraman into the water. They bite, too. Sea otters gobble crabs, shell and all, and their rear teeth are made for crushing.

Each otter has a distinct personality. Aquarium celebrities include Lootas, rescued from Alaska after her mother was killed by a boat, and Kodiak, a male Valdez oil spill survivor. Unable to find a commercial cargo flight to transport Kodiak northward, personnel put out a plea and found an entrepreneur who flies a French fighter jet as a hobby. Kodiak made the trip in less than two hours.

Lootas proved mischievous in 1999 when she caused eight hundred dollars in damage by battering on her aquarium window with a rock, but she's since proven a draw by giving birth to pups. Seattle's aquarium was the first to successfully breed sea otters in captivity, probably because its exhibit was designed to give the otters a view of approaching humans and thus relaxed them by eliminating surprise.

Like all mammals, otters are warm blooded, keeping their body temperature near one hundred degrees despite the cold water. Their milk has a fat content of nearly 25 percent, compared to 3 to 4 percent in cows and humans.

And do they have hair! They wear pelts that men sailed fifteen thousand miles for, fur of such softness, such suppleness, such luxury, and such sensuousness that Asian emperors spent fortunes to acquire it.

Unlike the river otter, the sea otter has almost no insulating fat or blubber. It instead spends four to eight hours of each day grooming its luxuriant pelt, blowing air bubbles into its fur to create an insulating layer between sea and skin. Its skin is so loose that it can pull its back fur around for attention from its muzzle. Sea otters roll, comb, nuzzle and smooth in a tireless effort to keep clean, because nothing less than their life is at stake. Any contamination such as oil or dirt punctures this cocoon and dooms the otter to hypothermia.

Sea otters float so well that they use their chest as a table, tucking spare food or primitive tools in the loose skin of their armpits. Gulls sometimes catch an otter snoozing during a lazy meal and swoop in to snatch a snack right from under its chin.

While sea otters prefer to feed in water just thirty to sixty feet deep, they have been measured diving as deep as three hundred and thirty feet and holding their breath for as long as five minutes. Their lungs are two and a half times larger than those of a similarly sized land animal, and their eyes can focus equally well both above and below water.

There are three subspecies of sea otters: the Russian, Alaskan, and Californian. To a layman, all look pretty much alike. The genetics of Washington's original population is unknown, but the state now has Alaskan otters in its Olympic Marine Sanctuary. After near extinction, the California otter population off Big Sur has increased to twenty-four hundred as of 2000.

The catastrophic annihilation of sea otters followed by their dramatic restoration has had a profound impact on the ecology of the Northwest coast, but just what that impact means remains uncertain. We know that otters are voracious eaters of shellfish. This may be a bad thing from both a human's and a clam's perspective. We also know that they eat sea urchins which prey on kelp. This can be a good thing.

Kelp forests (which at the height of the growing season can extend fronds at the rate of two feet a day) are a prime nursery for baby fish. They also absorb wave energy, protecting the coast from erosion. Sea urchins can clearcut and devour kelp forests at an average advance of a foot a day. Eliminate otters and you encourage urchins. More urchins mean you kill the kelp and hurt the fish. Introduce otters to eat the urchins, and the kelp comes back and with it more fish. Kelp itself is valuable, representing a $50 million industry in California. The algin that comes from kelp is used in a variety of food products from ice cream to beer. Kelp is also used as biodegradable surgical thread.

But humans also harvest urchins. So, are otters still necessary? Are they a seventeenth century anachronism or a rightful and keystone part of our ecology? Certainly a massive ecological experiment is underway. Senator Warren Magnuson's Marine Mammal Protection Act of 1972 has caused an explosive comeback of all kinds of marine mammals, including otters. And aside from an occasional black market sale attempted from poaching—otter pelts can bring two thousand dollars—the animal today is essentially unmolested.

As a result, biologists are waiting to see how things will balance out. Washington, with six hundred sea otters, is estimated to have the habitat capacity for up to two thousand. Will they stabilize? Will they collapse? Will other species adapt to their presence?

We may know soon. Although sea otters have only one pup at a time, they reach sexual maturity at three to five years and live in the wild about fifteen to twenty years. Each pregnancy lasts about six and a half months. Mothers care for their young as intently as fathers ignore them. At today's rate of increase, the coast could be filled with otters in a couple of decades. Management debate will increase with their numbers.

In the meantime, the return of the otter is encouraging. While the environment remains in severe trouble, animals like the sea otter offer important hope. The wolf, the whale, and the elephant all offer evidence that the wild can come back. So does the otter. Each success breeds more success.

So here's to the otter. Here's to a captivating creature that had completely disappeared for three human generations. Now you can see, on our Northwest coast, a sight that your grandparents missed.

That's progress.

Coyote, Crow, Raccoon, & Possum

*Can cope with zipper
& duct tape while
suspended*

FOR THE WILD AND SHY ANIMAL INHABI-
tants of the Pacific Northwest, our burgeoning urban cen-
ters such as Seattle and Portland must seem as impenetrable
as the storied walls of Constantinople, which withstood
assault for a thousand years. We fence out wildlife not just
with one wall but a thousand: barbed wire, backyard cedar,
brick, stone, and chain link. Our castles have not just one
moat but hundreds: moats of asphalt, patrolled by whizzing
two-ton sentries of steel that threaten to turn any infiltrators
into road kill.

Yet there's a cadre of animal Ninjas that doesn't just slip
by our fortifications, it sets up home inside. These Ninjas don't
just adapt, they thrive. These are the animals most like us:
smart, opportunistic, omnivorous, adaptable, and a wee bit
greedy. They see our gardens, dog-food dishes, and compost
piles fit for plunder.

Think of them as mythic heroes, or quest seekers in a computer game. Their leader is *coyote*, the central trickster of both
Native American legends and Roadrunner cartoons. He is a
silver shadow, swift and furtive, daring and hardy, smart and
persistent, with humor in his howl.

Their bandit is *raccoon*, who gets by with a combination of stealth, charm, and an intricate five-fingered paw that gropes in exploration like a pickpocket in Vegas. So plentiful is human food to this masked mischief-maker that there are probably twice as many raccoons per square mile inside metropolitan areas than outside them.

The brain of the operation is *crow*, whose bigger relative the raven was also prominent as a crafty character in Indian lore. This Einstein of birds is a gourmand of the discarded French fry, fallen Slurpee, and spilled Happy Meal. His numbers have exploded with urban sprawl. Communal, raucous, clever, and brooding, crows remind us of the dark side.

The nerd of the group is *possum*, a newcomer who arrived in the Northwest under its own power sometime in the 1960s. Looking like a giant rat with its naked tail and leaf-shaped ears, possum is like the erstwhile computer geek who is coming into his own. A primitive tropic marsupial long pushed around by newer mammals, this kangaroo relative has finally found a place to thrive: suburbia.

This quartet of animals is probably not among your most beloved. You may have had your pet cat devoured by coyote, your garbage raided by raccoon, your sleep broken by the noisy cawing of crow, and your crawl space colonized by possum. Yet each of these creatures is an urban reminder that we still share this planet with the wild.

It was only in 1992 that the sprawl of greater Seattle and the persistent presence of some species prompted King County to create its Urban Wildlife Program, directed by Kate Stenberg. "People would call to say [they] saw an animal and ask if they should be worried about it," she explains. After all, there are black bears in south Bellevue, beavers in Kirkland's Juanita Park, eagles in Seattle's swank Broadmoor neighborhood, fox in West Seattle—squirrels, gulls, deer, voles, and field mice. Oh my.

The job of people like Stenberg is to help us all get along. In community lectures she preaches a combination of tolerance, appreciation, and common sense. Attacks on humans are almost unheard of, but wild creatures do raid, chew, fight, yowl, and startle. One neighbor's cute wild visitor is another's overfed pizza predator.

Humans tend to insist that animals must adapt to us. Is it any wonder that the relationship is rocky? Stenberg suggests we look at King County from an animal's point of view, limiting the free handouts while connecting the county's wild lands into a coherent system of tree, brush, and marsh where they can feed themselves. Workfare! Conservatives should love it.

"King County still has really good habitat," she points out. "It's continuous from Lake Washington to the crest of the Cascades, through the Issaquah Alps. That's why we still have bears in Bellevue." The secret is to realize that the dead snags, mucky marshes, brushy ravines, and remnant woods are an animal paradise. "Let's look at our landscape as wildlife looks at it," she urges. Here's a test. If neighborhood kids are drawn to an overgrown snarl that grown-ups view as blight, chances are that animals love it too.

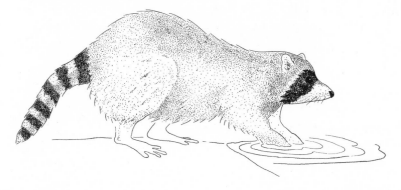

Of course we have to learn to appreciate our wild neighbors for what they are. Frankly, our Ninja band has an image problem. Yet these are some of the smartest and most adaptive of wild animals. They control pests, clean up after us, and, in the case of coyote, raccoon, and possum, stay out of our way by working the night shift.

Coyotes are a relative newcomers to western Washington and Oregon, following clearcut and farm from desert rangeland to lowland cities. Furtive and sly, they are the fastest in a zoological family that includes the dog, wolf, and fox. Coyotes are capable of sprinting at speeds up to forty miles per hour.

Like dogs, coyotes are social animals, sometimes running in packs. Resting by day and hunting at night, they can prey on animals as big as sick deer and as little as grasshoppers. They keep rodents in check, eat berries in season, and their fondness for garden melons earns them the nickname "melon wolf."

Coyotes breed from January to early March and produce a litter of about five to seven pups two months later. The young are born with eyes closed, weighing only eight ounces, but they double their weight in a week and run within a month. The fact that coyotes can reach sexual maturity in a year but live in the wild as long as fourteen years helps explain the failure of ranchers to eradicate them with poison, trap, and gun. Like the marauder of a horror sequel, they keep coming back.

Coyotes are also among the most wary, shrewd, and perceptive of animals, with superb hearing, sight, and smell. Capable of surviving great pain and severe wounds, they are a natural inspiration for their cartoon counterpart, who has survived endless explosions of Acme Dynamite. Wile E. Coyote may not win, but he persists. So too does his real-life counterpart.

If trickster coyote is furtive, the bandit raccoon has the arrogant presumption of the skilled panhandler. Catch them by flashlight banging through your garbage and they're unflappable, as apt to regard you as potential donor as threat. Chase them away and they'll waddle back in their own good time, so long as there's loot to be had.

Their name comes from the eastern Indian word *ara-koonen*, meaning "he who scratches with his hands." The term was spelled "Aroughcun" by Jamestown's Captain John Smith. He wrote about the beast as a source of food and fur in 1612.

It's not true that raccoons wash their food before eating, but it is true they will sometimes wet it to soften it. They also search for food in streams by feeling with their sensitive hands while looking elsewhere, ever watchful. Old-growth ecologist Chris Maser of Oregon State University tells a story about this habit in his book, *Mammals of the Pacific Northwest*. As a boy, Maser let loose a pet raccoon into his mother's bridge party. The animal first climbed up on one lady to seek the wax fruit on her hat and then, disappointed at the taste, went on to another and curiously fished with his paw down her cleavage.

The woman fainted from the attention.

The raccoon was sent back to the woods.

In a happier instance, police credited the species with saving a Cornell University student's life in 1990. Lisa Nelson fell seventy-five feet into a gorge but survived when she landed on a plump raccoon. The young woman recovered. The raccoon, sadly, succumbed.

In 1997 in Port Orford, Oregon, a conflict over raccoons in a strawberry patch resulted in animal lovers running "Rocky Raccoon" as a write-in candidate against an incumbent port commissioner. The human won, but not very convincingly: 345 votes to 301 for the raccoon, with another 180 voters declining to endorse either candidate.

Raccoons eat almost anything, enjoy sweets, and are adept at climbing. They den over the winter, not truly hibernating but losing up to 50 percent of their weight by spring. They breed after emergence and give birth about two months later to two or three kits, which are weaned after three months but don't become independent until the following year.

While there's no historical proof that Davy Crockett ever actually wore a coonskin cap, coon hunting has made humans the raccoon's worst enemy. We're also his best friend. Undeniably cute, raccoons have learned to associate us humans with food and our houses with winter shelter. As a result, their population is estimated to be fifteen times higher today than in the 1930s. Wild raccoons can live up to sixteen years, and their population explosions can result in damage to yards and rambunctious fighting.

Also thriving is the crow, a noisy and somewhat sinister-looking bird. Crows are so smart that Henry Ward Beecher once wrote: "If men had wings and bore black feathers, few of them would be clever enough to be crows."

Crows are corvids, a bird group that includes ravens, camp-robbing jays, and the farm-loving magpies of eastern Washington and Oregon. They live in family groups and have at least twenty-three distinct caws to communicate and to signal cooperation. They generally mate for life, serve as lookout for one another as they feed, and beckon each other to a free dinner.

They're also spooky. Crows have been associated since medieval times with graveyards and battlefields because they'll scavenge human remains. In England, a gravestone is sometimes called a ravenstone. A group of crows is called a "murder," based on the fallacious folk tale that crows gather to judge and murder an errant member of the flock. Crows have also been observed flocking to a "funeral," where as many as two hundred birds will mass briefly around a dead colleague before flying off.

Ravens are very similar to crows but are about one-third bigger and therefore are more comfortable in the wild. There are forty-two separate species of these two birds around the world.

Crows can mimic human speech as effectively as a parrot. They often return to the same tree to nest for year after year, and they exemplify family values. Several generations can combine to help build a nest, feed an incubating female, and chase away predators. Highly analytical, a crow can be observed reasoning as it figures out a way to break into a package or get plunder into its beak. Crows are also loud, bullying, and pushy. Sometimes dining on songbird eggs, they are the Mafia muscle of the bird world, expanding with urban sprawl.

The possum is the oddest of our quartet. One of the world's oldest surviving mammals, this pouched marsupial has survived unchanged for seventy million years. Migrating with human development from the south, possums showed up in

Seattle about the same time as the Beatles. Roughly the size of a cat, it is most commonly seen scuttling across the road at night like a giant rat, its pink eyes fiery in the headlights.

Possums don't inspire automatic love. Their rare scream is described by Maser as like that "of a stabbed woman." They look like a rodent that mutated at the Hanford nuclear reservation. Yet they are actually useful and rather clean neighbors.

The correct name is actually "opossum," again taken from an Indian word, and they are as solitary as crows are communal, coming together only to breed. If other animals are full of bluster, the possum thrives by lying low. It can't see, hear, run, or fight very well. It navigates mostly by smell. Coming out only at night, the possum will eat almost anything with its snout of fifty teeth—the most of any North American mammal—and survives quite nicely by opportunism, adaptability, and calculated faints. While possum will hiss and show its teeth when initially threatened, it falls into a comalike state and "plays possum" if a threat persists. This collapse often works: disconcerted enemies move on.

The possum is a strong swimmer, good climber, has an opposable thumb on its hind foot, is resistant to snake venom, and is immune to most contagious and viral diseases, including rabies. Because of this, and because it eat pests such as rats, mice, and roaches, the possum is a rather useful neighbor. Contrary to myth, however, a possum does not sleep while hanging from its tail. It snoozes in dark, cool, low places such as borrowed burrows, porches, decks, garages, and woodpiles.

Though its life span is short, three years at best, and though it is a frequent victim of the automobile, dogs, or the great horned owl, the possum prevails by a reproduction system that is fascinating. The young are born less than two weeks after conception and are smaller in size than a honeybee. They crawl, or more accurately "swim," on the mother's licked fur, traveling the perilous three inches from her genitals to her pouch. There the still-developing embryos fasten on one of thirteen nipples and remain attached for sixty to seventy days, growing to the size of a small mouse. The young then begin to leave the pouch, and within two more weeks they ride around on mother's back, clinging with feet and tail.

Soon, another crop of adult possums.

Because these suburban animals are so adaptive, it should be evident that we're not going to eliminate these neighbors in any landscape less paved-over than downtown Seattle or Portland. So how can we best coexist?

Wildlife official Kate Stenberg suggests that to limit animal numbers and damage, don't feed wild neighbors. Keep pet food, water dishes and cats indoors. Keep garbage lidded. Don't put food waste into compost piles. Pick up fallen fruit. Cover fishponds at night.

Second: don't let animals nest in your house. Search carefully for, and seal, any openings. If mammals have already taken up residence, try encouraging them to move on by putting ammonia-soaked rags or cotton balls in the attic or crawl space; they'll think it is urine from a rival tenant. A lit flashlight or a transistor radio tuned to a talk station might also help. It may be possible to see if they've left by powdering their exit with flour and watching for tracks. Once they've assuredly gone, seal up the exit.

On the other hand, you can encourage wildlife to behave like good relatives—to make brief, amusing visits. Start thinking of your yard as wildlife sanctuary. Landscape with native plants. They don't require fertilizer or pesticides and can resist our summer droughts. Build a layered habitat of ground cover, shrub, and tree. Consider leaving dead trees or logs some-where in the neighborhood if you have them: many species use dead wood. A small rock pile or thicket of wild roses can shelter animals. Insects are good, not bad, because they'll keep one another in check and provide food for a much wider vari-ety of birds and mammals than our Ninjas.

Finally, look at the broader environment. Creatures need roads just as people do, but their highways are corridors of trees and brush and swamp and stream. Can animals con-nect to neighboring wild areas or a neighbor's yard? Can they walk, swim or fly from alpine meadow to salt water?

We've chopped animal pathways to bits, but work is underway to piece some of these corridors back together. If that happens we may achieve a new balance with the natu-ral world, entertaining visits not just from our four Ninja infiltrators but from all kinds of Northwest wildlife. Imagine them edging down new pathways at night—and discovering to their surprise that the gates to our urban fortress have been thrown open.

SECRET & SMALL

Dirt

Scanning electron microscope purchased from Nancy by BHS (Bruce Claiborne & ?

ALL THAT IS SWEET AND FOUL IN LIFE — all that is sensual and gritty, alive and decayed, simple and complex, ancient and new, rich and poor, warm and cool — is represented by the squeeze of spring dirt in the palm of your hand.

Soil feels alive because it is. Open your fingers and you hold more microscopic creatures than there are humans on earth. Dig beneath the ground and you'll find more total life, or "biomass," under the surface than exists on top of it. Creatures of the earth range from worms to insects to fungus to bacteria, the latter found in drill holes thousands of feet deep. Scientists have estimated that the amount of living matter under each acre of dirt exceeds the bulk of ten draft horses.

You can smell some of this fecundity. The rich perfume of a freshly turned garden comes from Actinomycetes, a higher-level, moldlike bacterium. What you sniff is the life that truly drives the world. A clump of garden soil the size of a pea holds a billion bacteria.

We wash because these tiny creatures (a line of twenty-five thousand bacteria would stretch only an inch) can poison us: a spade routinely hauls tetanus microbes to the surface. Yet bacteria have also saved millions of lives: the drugs penicillin, streptomycin, tetracycline, and neomycin all come from the bacterial molds of the earth.

A square yard of Northwest forest soil contains about a quarter million insects of two hundred and fifty different species, representing as much diversity as the tropics. They graze on the billions of bacteria and on the one hundred coiled miles—yes, miles—of fungal thread found in every teaspoon of soil, says Andy Moldenke, the forest soil guru of Oregon State University. As they crawl along plant roots, feasting, these animals digest and defecate broken-down nutrients, which in turn become the primary food that root hairs can absorb.

It's a crucial partnership. Eliminate soil creatures, and plants would starve and die. Sterilize the soil, and we doom ourselves. "If you were a Martian ecologist who came to Earth, you would pay no attention to people and zebras and elephants and cats and all the things we think are important," Moldenke explains. "You would understand that all life nutrients come from organisms in the soil, and would concentrate on them. They are the crucible of biological diversity."

We Northwesterners are made of mud, in the sense that our food comes from soil. *Adam* is the Hebrew word for "wet clay," and the biblical story of his creation is echoed in modern science. Researchers have theorized that clay's microscopic pattern might have been the template, or pattern, on which Earth's earliest organisms assembled.

And we return to mud, or dust, in the sense that dirt— what author William Bryant Logan calls "the ecstatic skin of the earth"—is an endless recycling of all the life that has gone before. When historians sought to exhume the bones of colonist Roger Williams, they found that the roots of a nearby

apple tree had consumed the calcium of his bones and had
formed a pattern of living tissue that mimicked his skeleton.

Dirt is rot and regrowth. Charles Darwin estimated that
all the good soil on earth has been eaten and excreted by earth-
worms at least once. A worm will eat its weight each day,
decomposing dead plants into necessary nutrients. In good
compost, a single worm can produce a thousand offspring in
a single year. So beneficial are they in breaking down organic
debris and aerating soil that, according to Agriculture
Department experiments, a worm-populated plot grows veg-
etables at five times the rate of a wormless one. A study of a
Danish forest counted one and a half million worms, and six

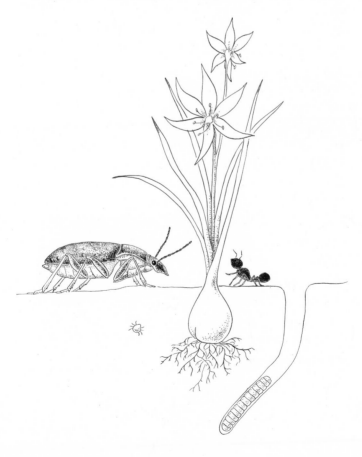

million worm channels, per acre. Northwest farm soils are relatively worm poor—we've tended to eliminate native worms, and European immigrants don't thrive here—and so our soils compact more than we would like, reducing their fertility.

Our language reflects our mixed feelings about the stuff underfoot. Scientists prefer the word "soil," a more refined term taken from the Latin root *solium*, meaning "seat," which includes organic material. The commoner "dirt" comes from the Old Norse *drit*, or excrement. Dirty looks. Dirty pictures. Dirty deeds.

To be "older than dirt" is to be old indeed. Yet the Earth recycles its crust so vigorously through erosion and vulcanism that two-thirds of the land we walk on has been made in just the last 4 percent of the planet's history. In much of the Northwest, dirt is far younger than that. Puget Sound basin residents live atop glacial deposits dropped by an ice sheet fewer than fourteen thousand years ago. Most of our terrain is dense hardpan—compressed by an ice sheet that was up to a mile thick—with a two- or three-foot looser layer of rock, sand, and clay dumped by glaciers on its top. Our organic soil "skin" is frequently only inches deep.

The rich farm soil of western Washington and Oregon frequently dates back just a few millennia. "Some of the best farming soils in the world are in our river valleys," notes Craig Cogger, a soil scientist at Washington State University's Puyallup extension research station. The land is young, rich, wet and, "unlike other farming areas, not very erodable." Nonetheless, we're losing these soils in a different way. "Basically, we're just paving them over." That's worrisome, because dirt is strategic. Our vast Midwest reserves of it made the United States a mecca for immigrants and an economic world power.

Egypt endured and Babylon fell because of dirt. The Nile floods replenished Egypt with fresh soil for five thousand years (until construction of the Aswan Dam) while the desert around the Tigris and Euphrates was so relentlessly irrigated by early civilization that it accumulated too many salts. Ancient empires turned into the wasteland of the Gulf War.

We could repeat Babylon's mistakes. Eastern Washington's farm fields have lost up to a third of their organic matter and microorganisms because of intensive farming, says Ann Kennedy, an Agriculture Department soil scientist in Pullman, Washington. Researchers are working hard to reverse the trend. They also track where dirt is going. Windblown soil is so rich with microbes that it can be traced back to its origin by the molecular "fingerprint" it carries of microbial remains. There's sharp debate about how best to maintain these bugs. Recent farming practice has been to plow under stubble to restore organics, but the extra plowing may do as much harm as good to the microscopic communities. New research suggests soil may actually do better if stubble is burned, the roots left undisturbed to decay naturally.

Dirt! Pioneers walked two thousand miles to get to Oregon's dirt. Hitler invaded Russia to seize Ukrainian dirt. Rome sowed the dirt of their Carthaginian archenemies with salt. William the Conqueror stumbled upon landing in England, and he seized the ground as an omen of victory. Columbus kissed the dirt. Symbolic stuff.

And, as Dr. Frankenstein would say, "It's alive!"

An ounce of clay is a miniature city with more rooms than New York City. What looks solid to us is, on the microscopic level, a comb of passageways made of tiny clay "bricks" or particles. A dirt cube half an inch on a side can contain ten thousand layers, stacked like the pages of a book and divided ten thousand times more by length and width. A book's pages have room for thousands of words, and an ounce of clay has room for millions of microscopic inhabitants. Unfold all the floors, walls, and ceilings of a lump of clay and the resulting surface layer of that ounce, scientists estimate, is ten acres.

Small wonder, then, that a thimbleful of dirt can be home to perhaps five billion bacteria, millions of single-celled protozoa, and hundreds of thousands of insects. The rich, sticky feel of good soil comes from the slimy bodies of billions of dead bacteria, smeared cells, and bug poop, a microbial manure. Appreciate it. So vital are these organisms to tree growth that researchers have recommended that logging be modified to conserve dirt, providing the microbes and insects necessary to the next generation of forest.

Without a microscope we are blind to soil's complexity. One square yard of lawn can contain ten billion root probes from its grass, each far slimmer than a human hair. A single rye plant puts out enough root filaments through the soil to reach six thousand miles, or twice across the United States.

Astounded by the persistence of weeds? A square yard of turned garden contains thirty thousand dormant weed seeds, most of which will never germinate but which will persist for years, waiting for a chance to sprout. (One arctic seed germinated after an estimated six thousand years of dormancy.)

Dirt is bustling with soil mites, miniature spiders, sow bugs, centipedes, beetles, maggot flies, worms, springtails, ants, and fungi. Snails crawl like tanks. Mammals plow. (One gopher was measured to have dug five hundred feet of tunnel in three months.)

Some of these organisms have formed beneficial partnerships. Douglas fir trees rely on mycorrhizal fungi to help their roots extract nutrients from the soil, and the tree feeds the fungus in turn. More than two thousand species of fungi have evolved to take advantage of this cooperative agreement, scientists estimate.

And some organisms are at war, as is detailed in the David Bodanis book, *The Secret Garden*. Ants are shiny from the antibacterial compound they squirt on their own shells. Competing plants can send poison gas attacks at each other through root tunnels. Willows excrete a pest-fighting poison that is also the chemical basis of aspirin. When pine beetles burrow into wood they deposit fungus spores that grow in the borehole nurseries, a "farm" that is eaten by the beetles. In defense, the pine injects the fungus with poison to kill the insects. Surviving beetles respond by converting the poison to a chemical signal to attract a mate. The pine hits back by sending its own signal to attract beetle predators. And so on.

These evolutionary conflicts have been developing for millions of years. Plants under attack by insects can release an alcohol scent that attracts a yellowjacket wasp that in turn eats the attacking bug.

Think of it this way: your yard is the Balkans, with rivalries that date into the distant past. You are NATO, intervening with shovel, hoe, spray, fertilizer, and seed. You may achieve your end. Or, you may accidentally destroy your friends and encourage your enemies. The whole exercise is temporary and hopeless, except that when left to itself, nature does achieve equilibrium. This is why a forested hillside can produce a more intricate garden than any of us dare achieve.

Down in the dirt, however, life isn't very sacred. Spores, seeds, eggs, and pollen are produced in fantastic numbers because individual life is so brief and fragile. One puffball on the forest floor can contain seven *trillion* fungal spores, each theoretically capable of producing another puffball. If all grew to full size, the volume of puffballs would be eight hundred times that of the earth.

In fact it is death—the decomposition of life into the chemical molecules that plants need—that keeps the whole thing going. And a good thing, too. For example, a single female aphid, if undeterred, could produce several million pounds of aphids in a summer. Beneficial insects like the ladybug are the superheroes that keep the Earth from turning into a monster movie. One ladybug can eat five thousand aphids in its lifetime.

It's hard for us to understand life at such a basic level because it's where biology meets chemistry and physics. There is a raucous symphony of chemical signaling going on that we can't sense. A tomato plant, for example can produce a muscle-freezing protein that can temporarily paralyze an attacking caterpillar, forcing it to fall off the vine. Geraniums pump out poison to kill mites. Trees "talk" to each other by emitting warning gases when attacked by insects, triggering the defenses of neighbors.

There is also a profoundly different "feel" to this miniature world. Ants are so small and light that they can climb straight upward and down because gravity exerts little pull on them. Fairy flies are so tiny that air, to them, feels as thick as water.

Dirt can also defy common sense. We might assume our

Northwest forests have particularly rich soils, given our particularly big trees. In fact, the needle and leaf litter dropped
by trees is consumed by decay about as fast as it is produced,
meaning forests usually have thin soil.

In fact, a tree needs only trace amounts of dirt to grow,
despite its extensive roots: it is a kind of magic act, a creation
of sunlight, water, and air that goes thunk. That's why you
can find big trees growing on cliffs of seemingly solid rock.
Yet without the recycling of crucial trace nutrients that goes
on in dirt, the tree dies.

The American prairies or Russian steppes, in contrast, can
build up soil sixty feet thick because their underground root
systems decay more slowly and build up layer by layer. But
when we break this sod, it erodes quickly. One study in
Missouri, for example, showed a third of that state's soil has
been lost to erosion since farming began.

Fortunately, we humans can improve soil as well. We can
hurry recycling along by composting garden waste. The
world's domestic animals produce two billion tons of manure
per year. (A single cow can contribute fifteen patties a day.)
We can fertilize, seed, and water. And we can "socialize" to
good effect. While the talking-to-plants fad has faded, we do
exhale necessary carbon dioxide onto any green and growing thing we chat, sing, or whistle to. Stroking it may release
ethylene gas, a signal for plants to produce fungus-fighting
poisons.

What we can't do is take dirt for granted. We don't really
know how long our farm soils will last. We don't really know
how many crops of trees we can grow. We may be clever enough
to sustain our soil. Or, like the Babylonians, we may not.

We do know that nature is on our side. Fourteen thousand years ago, half the Northwest was swept almost clean by

that glacial ice sheet almost a mile thick. Left behind was rock, sand, and silt as barren as the moonscape of Mount St. Helens. All that we see has come since then, creating a new Eden.

So breathe deep its pungent aroma. Appreciate natural renewal.

Just try not to think about the several thousand mites, spores, pollen bits, and bacteria that can be inhaled with every breath.

Stream Life

IMAGINE A PLANET OF BONE-CHILLING cold, a place with a shrieking current so fierce that its inhabitants have to cling to stones or risk being swept away, a world shaped like a ribbon that expands and contracts, warms and cools, and loses or gains oxygen as the seasons turn.

Imagine, in other words, a clear, cold stream—pools like champagne, a bottom that looks lacquered, and a purity that seems sterile.

Look again. Northwest creeks and rivers are long, sinewy ropes of life. When University of Washington graduate students flip over a couple of rocks in midwinter at a research site on Griffin Creek, east of Seattle, they routinely net a thousand swimming insects. The inhabitants range from an adult stonefly the size of a crisp Chinese noodle to baby mayflies no bigger than a comma.

A river, seemingly clear, hosts forests of algae, empires of bacteria, legions of insects, and underground strata of crayfish, clams, worms, and snails. Fish called sculpin skim the bottom, trout and salmon hide in the shadows, and frogs and salamanders emerge on the banks in spring. Tiny birds called dippers plunk themselves underwater on the coldest days, feeding on a cornucopia of bugs that we can barely see.

These biological ribbons are relatively rare: only one millionth of the world's water is in streams and rivers. (Ninety-nine percent is ocean water, and most of the rest Antarctic ice.) Despite their rarity, rivers are the environmentally vital threads that stitch ecosystems together. Animals feed, breed, and migrate along them.

Rivers are also coveted by humans. Worldwide, the amount of river water used for agriculture, drinking, and industry has soared four times since 1950.

We're just learning how important the last undisturbed creeks are.

Even in its natural state a stream is a chaotic place, always changing depth, temperature, course, and shape as it swells with rain and snowmelt and shrinks with drought. It's fed by falling vegetation and dying animals: a local trout was found with fifty ants in its belly, swallowed from a regiment that fell off a log. It's dammed with logs and branches. Gravel and sediment are flushed in and out.

Life has evolved to thrive in this uncertainty. Animals have developed ingenious strategies to stay anchored in the current, hatching in stages to straddle flood and drought. A comprehensive study of a creek in central Germany identified eleven hundred separate insect and worm species in just a few kilometers. That doesn't count algae, fungi, bacteria, plankton, mollusks, and fish.

We in the Pacific Northwest, however, are pushing this diversity to its limits. After a hundred years of "improving" streams by dredging, rip-rapping, channeling, clearing, and cleaning, we've increased the volume of winter floods, prolonged the period of summer drought, and turned meandering waterways of alternating pools and rapids into sediment-choked chutes that run like freeways to the sea.

"The major change we've made is to homogenize streams into a continuous riffle," explains Tom Sibley, a professor at the University of Washington's Center for Streamside Studies. He points to Griffin Creek, which lacks pools, waterfalls, sloughs, or rapids, as an example. "We don't know what normal is anymore."

Sibley's graduate student, Jamie Glasgow, is studying the two forks of the Tolt River, one of them dammed to supply Seattle with drinking water. "Life evolved to some swings," he said. "The question is whether we're increasing the swings." The volume of the Tolt's flow can jump one hundred times in a winter storm. What such a cataclysm does to the creatures within is barely understood. Glasgow has found that trout in the undammed fork of the river, with its more natural flow conditions, grow faster and bigger than those

below the dam. Presumably the insect life that feeds the trout is richer.

The question is not just academic. Some of the hundreds of millions of dollars being spent on salmon restoration in western Washington and Oregon will go toward putting streams back toward what they once were. How to do that is hotly debated.

The good news is that if we simply leave a strip of undisturbed land on either bank, forest and stream will combine to slowly put things back to rights. The bad news is that we don't really know how much land to leave. One study by the Tulalip Indian tribe near Everett showed clear benefits for buffers as wide as ninety feet, but uncertain gains after that. Seattle is proposing six-hundred-foot-wide buffers on its watershed streams. Farmers in northwest Washington's Skagit County have argued that twenty-five feet should be enough.

Attempts to set a government standard have run into a buzz saw of environmental and economic doubt. Since western Washington and Oregon are veined with creeks, the difference to timber companies, housing developers, road builders and farmers could run into billions of dollars.

We mismanage streams because they seem so alien. One of the first surprising things is that their ceatures *like* that shocking cold. It helps them rest and breathe. Water molecules include atoms of oxygen, but the oxygen is so tightly bonded that animals can't breathe it. Instead they depend on oxygen from the air that diffuses into water from waves and rapids, or oxygen produced by water plants or algae. As a result, oxygen is about thirty times less available in fresh water than air. The diving beetle gets around this problem by carrying an air bubble down with it, surfacing when its natural scuba tank gives out. Other stream inhabitants aren't so ingenious. To add to their problem, as water warms it loses its ability to hold oxygen. Meanwhile, the metabolism of cold-blooded fish, insects, mollusks and worms speeds up. Clear-cutting a stream, thus robbing it of shade, can raise its temperature an average of six to seven degrees centigrade. Each degree rise accelerates a fish's respiration rate by 10 per-cent. Warm a creek, and to a panting fish it's equivalent to being locked in a trunk, stuck on an accelerating treadmill, or marooned on the summit of Everest.

Streams also like to take their time to get to the sea, gob-bling, restoring, and flooding land as they go, making side channels and swamps. From the air they look rubbery and indecisive, and we humans think the way to improve them is to straighten them out. What a stream is doing, however, is losing its own too-abundant energy and restoring its struc-ture by going the long way.

When Germans decided to hurry floodwaters downstream by straightening the Rhine in 1817, for example, the suddenly impatient river cut its channel twenty feet deeper, drying up orchards and wells. Straightened streams gather fewer nutri-ents from the land and have fewer pools and sloughs. Their less hospitable bottoms harbor fewer insects and fish.

Thirty years ago, Washington's land managers ordered log-ging companies to remove tree trunks and wood debris from creeks, believing the mess choked off habitat for fish. Now we pay loggers to put trees in because they slow a river's flow, create aerating pools and ripples, and support a skin of bac-teria, fungi, and plankton that are the base of the stream's food chain and oxygen supply.

It all starts with slime, you see. Ever tried to wade a swift stream? The rocks are slicker than a greased cookie sheet, and the reason is that they support a "biofilm" of the same stuff that grows on wet logs. This is the river's garden: the almost microscopic plants and animals that larger insects and worms eat before becoming food themselves. Bacteria are so small that they are protected from turbulence by the relatively thick sludge of surrounding water molecules; to them, swimming is like corkscrewing through honey or tapioca pudding. At their scale, there can be millions of bacteria in a thimbleful of water. Single-celled protozoa, microscopic creatures more complex than bacteria, also exist in countless numbers. One study showed that a streambed the size of a moderate room could grow a pound of protozoa a year. Greenish-brown algal scum is more visible and serves the same function as a forest. It converts sunlight, water, and carbon dioxide into sugar and oxygen through photosynthesis. Even big stream plants, vital in their own right, are covered by this productive slime. Stroke the stem of a lily pad and you bulldoze a microscopic garden.

This tiny life has evolved ingenious strategies. Diatoms, which are single-celled algal plants, encase themselves in crystal greenhouses. Made of silica, which is the same material found in glass, the tiny boxes protect the microscopic plant while allowing sunlight and selected molecules to come inside.

More food comes into the stream from fallen leaves that are rapidly colonized by bacteria and fungi. An alder leaf leaches so many nutrients so quickly that it can lose a quarter of its weight during its first twenty-four hours in the water. The rest is devoured within weeks. Dead animals contribute to the cycle. Spawned-out salmon fertilize plants and feed scavenging animals. The water is also full of "dissolved organic matter," or the molecules of plants and animals that have been completely broken down.

In sum, a stream may look and taste clean, but you're really drinking thin organic soup in a dilute solution of calcium bicarbonate, a kind of salt. If the water flows by farms or fertilized lawns, you can count on a good dose of nitrogen as well. One study in Ireland showed that a third of the nation's fertilizer is washed into its streams before feeding any plants.

Griffin Creek, which flows through a Weyerhaeuser tree farm, was originally logged to its banks in the early 1900s. At the second harvest in the 1980s, the company left alone a strip of young alder and cedar that had grown up on either bank. As a result the creek is healthier than many foothill streams, supporting coho salmon that swim to it from the Snoqualmie River.

At the encouragement of the company, scientists from the University of Washington are studying the creek to improve it even more. Beaver dams upstream that trap and pond the floodwaters have been left undisturbed. Whole logs and bundles of small poles have been put in the stream to see if they help to create pools, eddies, and small falls. The latter help push oxygen into the water.

The complexity of Griffin Creek begins to become apparent when scientists stretch a fine mesh net in the current and let it strain water. In less than an hour it yields a fistful of floating debris: tree needles, pieces of leaves, floating insects, and even a stray crayfish. The water is full of insects. Species such as mayflies, caddis flies, and stoneflies spend most of their life underwater, breathing through gills, before emerging into the air as adults to breed and die. The dance of insects observed above the water in summer gives some idea of the density of juveniles growing below the surface in winter.

Their life cycle keeps stream biology in equilibrium. Adults tend to fly upstream to deposit their eggs, helping repopulate stream areas from which insects have drifted downstream. Their wing color changes after egg laying, and Glasgow has discovered that trout prefer the color of bugs that have already laid their eggs—an instinct that helps ensure fish a future food supply.

A stream is bigger than it looks. The water can extend below the bed we see for several feet, creating an underground river called the *hyporheal zone*. Insects, worms, crayfish and freshwater mollusks inhabit this subsurface world. The water also extends sideways; when you walk on a riverbank, part of the stream may be flowing beneath your feet. So wide is this zone that aquatic insects have been found a quarter mile from Montana's Flathead River. They swim underground to the edges of the buried river before popping to the surface.

Insects have also evolved a variety of strategies for living in the current. Some species of waterbug skate on top of the water, using its surface tension like a film of ice to keep from going under. Down at the bottom of a stream, current greatly slackens a few millimeters from the rocks because of friction, and so insects crawl in this calm zone. Mayfly larvae have a streamlined shape to help the current slip by them, and a sucker on their belly to hold onto the rocks.

Caddis flies anchor themselves with silk. Like the fibers produced by silkworms or spiders, this silk is stronger than steel for its width and weight and is used to build a house to protect its occupant. Sand, tiny rocks, conifer needles, bits of wood, and scraps of leaves may all be wound together with the silk to make a kind of cocoon. Looking like bits of sticky twig, these can often be found stuck to river rocks.

Many of these insects graze like contented cows. There are scrapers that mow the rocks, collectors that filter out whatever is flowing by, shredders, piercers, predators, and so on.

Fish are usually the sole occupants of the water column itself, and to other stream inhabitants they are like vast, predatory blimps floating overhead to feed on the bottom or snatch at insects on the surface or in the air. Many fish are homebodies. Brown trout and arctic grayling tend to stick to the same fifty or one hundred feet of river.

Salmon, in contrast, migrate to and from the sea. Some species like coho spend the first year or more of their life in a stream. Chinook leave quickly. When salmon return to spawn and die, their carcasses feed not only the big animals like bear and eagle but also the tiniest bacteria. A dam or dike or culvert that cuts off this migration starves a stream of nutrients.

Learning how streams work takes patience and gumption. The water is freezing to scientists, the brush and insects miserable, and the climate dark and rainy half the year. Much of the biological activity goes on at night. Yet a healthy stream becomes a core refuge and corridor of biological diversity. Restoring it is one of the most dramatic environmental improvements possible and, with time, one of the easiest.

The formula: keep a forested buffer on either side of the waterway and then leave the whole thing alone.

Mosses & Lichen

AMERICANS ARE TAUGHT THAT NEWER IS better. Electronics, automobiles, kitchen colors, politicians, food fads, celebrities, fashion: out with the old, in with the new! It's tempting to think that nature works the same way. Mammals are sprightlier than reptiles, right? We big-brained humans are one of the newer species on the planet and top dog to boot, right? Old, simple, and small is for losers. Right?

Trouble is, the most numerous and widespread organisms on the planet are often the earliest and most modest. You want to talk numbers? Your own skin hosts about six hundred million bacteria that predate everything. Genealogy? There's mold in your bathroom that can trace an ancestry a thousand times longer than our entire species. Variety? There are more than a million species of beetle.

Sure, plenty of creatures have gone extinct. Plenty more have taken every disaster nature can throw at them and are still around. This means that a walk in the woods can be a visit to Jurassic Park. "Ancient forest" hardly begins to describe the antiquity of many of the plants that are still our contemporaries. Conifer trees predate the earliest dinosaurs by about sixty million years. Those knee-high horsetails are even older; they once reared sixty feet high. Flowering shrubs came much later, but *Tyrannosaurus rex* could still have stopped to smell them, if so inclined. World of the dinosaurs? The plant side lives on in Northwest forests.

Midwinter is a good time to tour Jurassic Park. It's then we can easily see the ferns, shrunken back from their Coal Age fifty-foot glory but still doing quite well. It's then that some of the earliest, simplest, most "primitive" and surprisingly successful of plants glow in our gloom with a joyous, electric-green vigor. I refer, of course, to the mosses.

We Northwesterners know all about moss. I pointlessly battled it for fifteen years in my own front lawn in a futile campaign to favor non-native grasses. Moss is a splendid green carpet all by itself, maintenance free. Nonetheless I poisoned it, coated it with lime, raked it, mowed it, picked it, aerated it, and finally came to terms with it only by moving away to a house in the woods that has no lawn—but still has plenty of moss.

And no wonder. Moss has been around for 400 million years. There are an estimated eight hundred species of moss in the Pacific Northwest, and twenty thousand in the world. A single Northwest tree can host fifty different kinds. The west slope of the Olympics grows moss at the rate of three tons, dry, to the acre. Independent contractors bag the stuff and export it to florists around the world at a wholesale price of about forty dollars for two and a half cubic feet. We generate moss the way Hollywood does hype.

Moss grows everywhere, and scientists mean *everywhere*. Grant Sharpe, a retired forestry professor at the University of

Washington, did his doctoral dissertation on Olympic mosses and found one kind that appears to grow on nothing but bear scat.

The Pacific Northwest's unofficial moss lady is Nalini Nadkarni, a scientist and instructor at The Evergreen State College in Olympia. Before getting married, she slept a year and a half on a bed of moss (no sheets) that she had packed into an old fiberglass toboggan shell. The moss, maintained with an occasional misting, stayed spongy and alive. "It was a wonderful place to sleep," she said, especially after the slugs and bugs moved out.

For the city of Olympia's annual Parade of the Species, Nadkarni made a cloak of moss by sewing the stuff onto a cape of lace, using dental floss. The cloak is warm, green and very much alive. Exposure to a little rain both waters and feeds it.

Nadkarni first attracted fame and notoriety by figuring out a way to use climbing gear to scale the trees of old-growth forests, a technique later adopted by eco-protesters. She discovered that big leaf maples have a marriage with moss. The trees provide the growing platform, and the mosses decompose into such a handy food source that the maple branches put out roots that burrow into the moss to feed.

Now she's at it again, trying to determine if the commercial collection of mosses pioneered in the 1980s is stripping forests too completely, too fast. Preliminary studies suggest moss grows back slowly, often not recolonizing a bare spot for a decade. Her classes make "moss milkshakes" of milk and moss which they paint onto some of Evergreen's concrete walls to see how quickly moss establishes itself on a new surface.

Shag moss buyer Bob Hayes, who operates a business on the Olympic Peninsula called Hohgrown, says his product can grow back in five years or so. He may be right, or wrong. Scientific studies have estimated growth rates of moss from one to thirty percent a year — an enormous variation that has yet to be narrowed in a field where researchers are few.

The issue is potentially important. Not much of anything eats low-nutrition moss, but it's important as a nesting site for rare birds, as a nutrient source for other plants, as a soil builder, and as a water absorber. At least six kinds of local mosses appear to grow only in old-growth forests, making them another potential legal ally of the spotted owl in discouraging logging of that ecosystem.

Plus, moss is pretty. In his book *Moss Gardening*, former Seattle landscaper George Schenk calls mosses "misunderstood friends, better garden prospects than a sulky crop of grass." The moss garden at Saihoji in Japan, planted in the fourteenth century, covers a spectacular four and a half acres. The "Hall of Mosses" walk in the Hoh rainforest of Olympic National Park is one of the tourist must-sees in the Pacific Northwest.

To better appreciate the felt-like beauty of moss, take a magnifying glass or hand lens and look closely. Some moss leaves look like feathers, others like ferns, others like palm trees. A mossy rock is a forest in itself.

Like many successful organisms, moss is pretty simple. It doesn't flower. It doesn't turn pretty colors in the fall. It doesn't flutter in the breeze. And yet it's not quite as dull as it looks. Moss has a complex sex life. It snatches food out of thin air. It goes dormant and then comes back to life. It can absorb two hundred times its weight in water.

Mosses were some of the first plants to colonize land. Like their fancier cousins, they know the trick of converting sunlight, water, and air into food, and they are mostly green because of the internal chlorophyll that accomplishes photosynthesis. Unlike higher plants, they're not vascular, meaning they don't have tubes to carry water and nutrients. They absorb what they need through osmosis, from cell to cell.

Mosses are epiphytes, or air plants. They don't need a bed of soil to grow. Raindrops form around a speck of dust, Nadkarni explains, and this falling dust and water is all that most mosses need to thrive. Rain delivers nitrogen, calcium, and magnesium. Fog and mist are even better: the ratio of fertilizing grit to water is higher in the smaller droplets. During summer drought a moss simply shuts down, curling up and going dormant, and the closure of its leaf makes it look brown. When water returns, it opens up, switches back on, and photosynthesis resumes.

Moss is tolerant of weak sunlight, meaning it can grow where other plants give up. It is indifferent to cold. It can grow on vertical surfaces and upside down because it doesn't have true roots, but rather wisplike rhizoids that help hold it to stone, wood, dirt, asphalt shingle, and concrete. For the most part, this invasion is fairly harmless to the host, though moss can be a maintenance nuisance by holding water that encourages other decomposing organisms.

This simplicity gives moss enormous advantages. We die of thirst in days and of hunger in weeks. Moss can go decades. We succumb if punctured, but you can rip moss into shreds, and the bits and pieces left are often capable of reestablishing themselves. We've transformed the planet to feed ourselves, yet all moss needs is a little rain. We build airplanes, but moss spores can cross oceans on the wind.

Moss sex is remarkably complex. Clumps of moss consist of both male and female plants that have an alternating generation method of reproduction: the green leafy moss produces a spore case, and the spore parent produces a green leafy moss.

Male plants, which look like tiny cups, release sperm that literally swim to females during a rain, using tiny hairs as oars. The fertilized female—which has narrow stalklike leaves sheltering the eggs—then produces a wiry stem topped with a spore cap, an upright pod that holds the individual moss cells, called spores. You can see these sometime in the spring. The cap breaks open and the spores disperse on the wind.

If the spores fall where it is wet, they begin to grow by putting out a mass of threads about an inch across which then bud into tiny stalks and slender leaves. Moss is adaptable and ubiquitous, growing wherever it is wet, from arctic tundra to tropical rainforest.

Moss is not very nutritious but it has long been used for bedding, insulation, and even bandages. Nadkarni notes that sphagnum, or peat moss, was used as a wound dressing during World War I because its acids help fight bacteria. This is the same moss that we spade into our gardens because it holds water like a sponge.

Moss is so common it's overlooked. The Forest Service and the National Park Service have a hard time recruiting naturalists who know anything about it. Nadkarni estimates that there are perhaps twenty people in Washington State who can identify an appreciable number of Northwest moss species. Her college has no course on nonvascular plants.

If moss is humble, the look-alike lichen is even more so. Though the two are frequently confused with each other, they are very different: a lichen is a partnership between a fungus, which provides structure and protection, and an alga, which feeds the enclosing parasite through photosynthesis. Some botanists call it a master-slave pairing. In general, the whitish stuff is lichen and the greenish stuff is moss, but confusion is common. Reindeer moss is a lichen, for example. Spanish moss is neither a moss nor a lichen, but a flowering air plant, or bromeliad. Lichens can form beardlike growth that hangs from branches. They decorate bark. Orange, yellow, and red lichens brighten the dull basalt cliffs of Grand Coulee as colorfully as paint, and Nadkarni has made lichen jewelry.

Lichen is even older than moss, dating back a billion years. Scientists have proposed that the biblical manna from heaven that rained down on the Israelis in the Sinai might have been lichen blown off desert mountaintops, a phenomenon observed in modern times. Today, lichens come in fifteen thousand species and are an important colonizer of raw rock. Their threadlike roots produce a weak acid that allows them to burrow into stone. Then they swell with water, fracturing the rock surface. This first step in soil formation paves the way for other plants.

We may pay little heed to moss and lichen today, but they once ruled the world. They've stepped aside without stepping out. Just as print made room for radio, radio for television, and television for the Internet, lichens and mosses have made room for subsequent ferns, trees, flowers, and grasses.

 We don't have dinosaurs in our woods but we do have their landscape. Get down on your hands and knees and you're back at the dawn of time.

Mosquitoes

RECOGNIZE THIS BUNCH?
The females are bloodsuckers.

The males wander in aimless circles while they whine for mates.

Both sexes spend most of their time sitting around.

Nobody likes them.

But no, we're not talking about your relatives, or your co-workers, or the cast of a bad sitcom. We're talking mosquitoes, the one bit of wildlife with which virtually everyone has intimate contact in the Pacific Northwest. They were here before us, by a margin of about 200 million years. They'll probably be here long after we're gone. And they've got us outnumbered: on any given day, scientists estimate, there are a hundred *trillion* mosquitoes in the world. That's nearly two thousand per person.

Why? Has any slap-weary camper not wondered, as dusk brings a climax of mosquito torment, how a creature so obnoxious can be so successful? Simply put, mosquitoes have been perfecting their shtick since the time of the dinosaurs. True, their brains are smaller than the period following this sentence. They don't really think. They're not self-conscious. But they're brilliantly programmed to make more mosquitoes. For females, that means obtaining blood from another animal — you! — to get the protein needed to develop her eggs. And she does. Mosquitoes may fly slower than a steady walk, but they can fly sideways and backwards. They are so light (it can take twenty thousand to make a pound) that the wind from your slapping palm often blows them out of harm's way. You can spray, swat, zip, and hide all you want. Ultimately, the mosquito wins.

"Why me?" is the next most common question. Why can a virtuous, kind, comely, and brilliant honor-student-eagle-scout-homecoming-queen type like yourself get eaten alive (researchers in Canada once allowed themselves to be exposed to a swarm and were bitten nine thousand times in one minute, an experience which calls into question the entire scientific method), while your disgustingly unbitten and unsympathetic camping partner can only say: "What mosquitoes?"

Mosquitoes are attracted to us by the carbon dioxide we exhale (hint: don't breathe) as well as skin oils, lactic and folic acids, body heat, and lotions. But why some people attract more mosquitoes than others, and why some react more severely to bites than others, remains a scientific mystery. The best you can do is swat. Not the mosquito. Whack the insensitive dolt who blithely insists, "They're not so bad." It will make you feel better, I promise.

Mosquitoes in the tropics are a dead-serious business. Humans spend hundreds of millions of dollars each year trying to control their numbers. By transmitting malaria, yellow fever, encephalitis, dengue fever, and fibriasis, mosquitoes have killed more humans than has any other group of animals on Earth. "Every year, two million kids die of malaria

in Africa alone," says Leonard Munstermann, an entomolo-
gist at Yale who has studied the pests globally.

But mosquitoes just transport disease, they don't create it,
and generally they don't infect humans in regions where
humans aren't already infected. So back home in Connect-
icut, Munstermann feeds his study subjects by inserting his
hand in their cage and allowing himself to be bitten up to a
hundred times. He says making himself mosquito-feed for his
research is easier than the paperwork required to keep larger
lab animals, and he's been bitten so often that he's developed
an immunity to the mosquito saliva that causes those itchy
bumps.

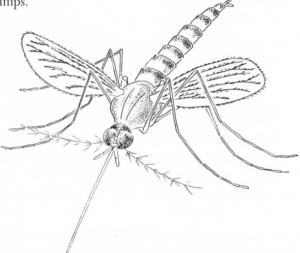

Malaria has been largely eradicated from the United
States and other developed temperate countries, not just by
spraying, but by screens, air conditioning, and health care.
Such simple measures cut the chances for a mosquito, in her
brief lifetime, to bite an infected person or animal and then
transmit the disease to an uninfected one. Mathematically,
mosquito-borne diseases can slowly be stamped out. But mos-

quito resistance to pesticides, bans on the use of DDT, and inconsistent control programs have let malaria and other mosquito diseases make a recent comeback in the developing world.

This is one more reason to be glad if you live west of the Cascade Mountains, a region which generally doesn't have poisonous snakes, killer bees, or kudzu. Pacific Northwest mosquitoes are pesky but relatively harmless. Of the world's known thirty-five hundred mosquito species, our region has a known total of forty-three.

Not that this relative paucity of species guarantees low numbers. Alaska has only thirty-two kinds of mosquitoes, but they're so thick on the Alaska tundra that I once witnessed a mosquito-slapping contest at a scientific research camp. Hundreds were killed with each whack, an act of prowess not only futile but necessitating the diligent washing of one's hands.

While Pacific Northwest bug counts are relatively low, Terry Whitworth, owner of Whitworth Pest Control in Tacoma, has seen hatchings of mosquitoes so horrible in coastal estuaries of Washington State that people in Aberdeen and South Bend have been driven indoors. Whitworth, who is armed as well with a Ph.D. in entomology, has been at war with the mosquitoes of Renton's Panther Creek wetlands, near Seattle, for twenty years. And the mosquitoes always come back. Always. They've been found at altitudes as high as Mount Rainier and in mines half a mile deep.

With thirty-five hundred species, generalizing about mosquitoes is as misleading as generalizing about human race, gender, age, or neighborhood. I'm going to generalize anyway. Mosquitoes were called "midges" in English until the sixteenth century. The newer name can be traced from the

Latin *musca*, or "fly." *Mosquito* or "little fly" came from the Spanish and Portuguese, who found more of the pests than they wanted to as they explored the New World.

Mosquitoes are indeed part of the insect order that includes flies, or insects with only two wings instead of four. No-see-ums and black flies are close relatives that bite. Crane flies, house flies and deer flies are more distant ones.

Most, but not all, mosquitoes lay their eggs in water. They hatch into larvae that feed on bacteria and plant material until they pupate and emerge as flying adults. Adult mosquitoes live an average of only two weeks.

The mission of adults is to produce the next generation. Those seemingly aimless clouds of orbiting, whining mosquitoes are male adults trying to attract a female by sound. She flies into the cloud, mates in midair in a coupling that usually takes from four to forty seconds (some love bugs have been recorded taking up to an hour, however), and then fights off any further attention. One mating gives her sperm enough for several batches of eggs, and slapping mosquitoes doesn't make much of a dent in their population because each surviving female can lay several hundred eggs per batch.

Equally bad news is that most females need blood from another animal to provide the necessary nutrients for their eggs to develop. Any animal will do. Research suggests mosquitoes prefer birds but will feed on mammals or frogs and will even bite between the scales of a snake. We humans don't have the best blood but we're conveniently big, smelly, and slow.

(Males make do with plant juices and flower nectar, which I thought made my own gender look uncharacteristically good—until scientists told me the guys are so single-minded that they'll keep mating even if their head is removed. Some things in life, it seems, are constant.)

The female mouth has not one but six piercing parts, called *stylets*. Four are like tiny saws, ripping open your skin to raise blood. One stylet injects saliva that keeps your blood from coagulating. This is the substance that itches, and scratching tends to push the saliva into a wider and wider skin area, worsening the bite. The sixth stylet is a trough. The others wrap around it to make a tube, and the female pumps about a millionth of a gallon of blood into her abdomen until it stretches taut, telling her enough is enough. At that rate, it would take more than a million mosquito bites to drain you.

Mosquitoes can also bite more than once. That's how they transmit disease, but only some human diseases can survive inside a mosquito's digestive tract. AIDS is not one of them.

While we pay attention to mosquitoes only when they attack, the insects spend most of the day doing nothing, needing only an hour a day to feed. They rest in cool, shady areas because their bodies are so tiny that they can rapidly dehydrate in bright sun. That's why dusk is a favorite feeding time and shade is a common habitat.

In theory, it should be easy to avoid mosquitoes. Since they fly slower than most people walk, any good breeze will force them to take cover. Most mosquitoes travel only a mile or two from their birthplace. Find a big enough parking lot and you've left most of them behind. West of the Cascades, however, mosquitoes can be hatched almost anywhere. Backwaters, bogs, small woodland pools, tree cavities, and snowmelt puddles can all harbor eggs. So can old tires, forgotten pails, birdbaths, and wading pools. A wet spring followed by a hot spell triggers ideal breeding conditions in the region. In the mountains some mosquitoes lay eggs on the moist undersides of leaves. The eggs stay dormant all winter, surviving amid the snowy landscape because of an antifreeze compound. Then they hatch out in springtime mush.

Mosquito numbers are highest where there is a combination of moisture and heat, helping to explain the huge numbers in soggy Alaska, with its endless summer days, and in humid Florida. (Munstermann, who has been bitten almost everywhere on Earth, says the mosquitoes of the Florida Keys are the most aggressive he's ever encountered.) In the Pacific Northwest, mosquitoes are often at their worst in the irrigation districts east of the Cascades, where farm water and sun can make them a plague in Moses Lake or the Tri-Cities.

While most mosquitoes live fast and die young, a few adults overwinter in cellars, barns, caves, or hollow logs, forming their own antifreeze compounds to survive. These adults plus some dormant eggs get the cycle going again the following spring. And it works. Mosquitoes have survived mass extinctions, Ice Ages, shifting climates, and drifting continents. No disaster movie scares them.

For a while, humans seemed to have a solution: drain the swamps and spray with DDT. Then the ecological importance of wetlands was recognized and the ecological dangers of DDT were documented. Mosquitoes today are controlled in water and air by bacterial spray that targets larvae, by growth regulators, by the pesticide malathion (which breaks down rapidly but still has the problem of killing beneficial insects as well as harmful ones), by petroleum products that suffocate the breathing tubes of larvae, or by introduced predators such as South American guppies.

For individuals, the most effective mosquito repellent is

a chemical called DEET (N,N-diethyl-meta-toluamide), used in varying percentages in different sprays and creams. DEET really isn't good for us, however. It should never be put on infants, and children should not use repellents with more than a 10 percent concentration.

Experts don't support claims that Avon's Skin-So-Soft, citronella candles, garlic, spicy foods, vitamin B1, Bounce fabric softener sheets, sonic devices, or geraniums are very effective against mosquitoes. Bug zappers are actually counterproductive. Rod Crawford, insect curator at Seattle's Burke Museum, cited one experiment where almost fourteen thousand insects killed by zappers were analyzed. Only thirty-one of them were mosquitoes, while nearly two thousand were beneficial insects that prey on the pests. Burning of mosquito coils may help slightly, but these and citronella candles should only be used outdoors. Research *does* suggest that mosquitoes are less attracted to light-colored clothing, are neutral about blue and khaki, and home in on black and red.

Keeping your head in a plume of campfire smoke also helps.

Surefire is a move to Iceland. That island has snow and volcanoes but no mosquitoes.

What good are these insects? Mosquito larvae eat bacteria and debris in wetlands, helping clean the water. They are so numerous that they are important feed for fish, birds, frogs, insects, spiders, and even other mosquitoes. They do help pollinate plants.

And they change history.

European colonizers were kept out of most of tropical Africa by malaria until the nineteenth century, when quinine (which is no longer effective against malaria) was developed. The Panama Canal was completed by the United States instead of France because mosquito-borne diseases that killed twenty thousand had defeated the French engineers. A team of American doctors led by W. C. Gorgas, and including Dr. Walter Reed, temporarily eradicated nearby mosquitoes so the canal could be completed.

And mosquitoes are arguably part of the reason that residents of Washington State don't have to know the words to the anthem, "Oh, Canada." My reasoning? Washington wound up in the United States in part because Lewis and Clark helped lay an early American claim there. Lewis and Clark were sent to the Pacific Northwest as a result of the Louisiana Purchase. Napoleon sold French holdings in North America to the United States because he gave up on plans to establish an empire here. And Napoleon gave up his ambitions in America because his expeditionary army of thirty-three thousand that landed in Haiti (and was supposed to go on to New Orleans and the Mississippi) was wiped out by malaria and yellow fever, diseases that were delivered by mosquitoes.

Mosquitoes, of course, seem pretty modest about their role in human events. Their only real goal is to reproduce. They are biological robots, DNA-replication machines. Of course, some scientists contend that when you strip away all the vanities, ambitions, maneuvers, and angst of human life, that's all we are as well.

So swat without remorse in our Northwest, lather up discreetly with DEET—and philosophize that the endlessly irritating mosquito, whining in your ears, perhaps has something important to tell us about ourselves.

Spiders

THIS ESSAY MAKES TWO POINTS, ONE OF
which you may not want to know and the other you may
not wish to believe. First: the Pacific Northwest is infested
with spiders, eight hundred and fifty identified species and
counting. There are spiders in the dirt, spiders on bushes, spi-
ders in trees and rotting logs, spiders on clearcuts and meadows, spiders in attics, spiders under your house, spiders
around your deck, and probably, in autumn, spiders in your
bathtub. Most are too tiny to be casually noticed, but look
carefully. A square meter of Northwest forest floor typically
contains one hundred to two hundred spiders.

Happy camping!

Second: spiders are our friends. This latter point requires
some explanation. Most spiders, after all, have fangs. They
have venom. They are predators, dining exclusively on other
animals by sucking out their flesh. They are eight-legged,
hairy, alien-eyed, and they vomit digestive juices. They scuttle so fast that a large house spider is six times quicker, for its
size, than the fastest human sprinter on Earth.

That's all to the good, explains Washington's Spider Man,
Rod Crawford. He is curator, or overseer, of the spider col-

lection at the University of Washington's Burke Museum. It's the second largest repository of arachnids on the West Coast, after that of the California Academy of Sciences, and Crawford helps fill it. Entering the field with pith helmet, spider net, and a surplus ammo belt stuffed with vials, he routinely discovers new species in the Northwest. In his bearing, purpose, persistence, and skill, he is the quintessential collector.

On an outing to Beljica Meadows near Mount Rainier, Crawford increased his count of species collected at that particular location from sixteen to twenty-four in just a few hours. Wolf spiders, so named because they chase down prey instead of using webs, scrambled through the grass. Orb weaver spiders rappelled from hemlock boughs. A sweep of net through huckleberry bushes released a rain of spiders. A probe of a rotted log turned up still more. Crawford's sharp eye turned a mountain meadow into a scene from *Arachnophobia* within minutes.

We ate our lunch standing up.

Crawford spent his childhood collecting butterflies in Des Moines near SeaTac, became fascinated with spiders during a high-school zoology course, and spent his first summer as a student at the University of Washington combing available spider literature in the library. "That was my idea of fun in those days, and it still is," he remarks. His job is to identify, preserve, and label the region's spiders, to field phone calls from worried or perplexed locals, and to fight the good fight against spider myths. For example, he has been bitten by a tarantula spider when coaching a local television host on how to handle the beasts, but the bite did nothing but raise a couple drops of blood. He thinks most "spider bites" are actually misdiagnosed, knows the vast majority of spiders are harmless, and despite claims to the contrary, is skeptical that any

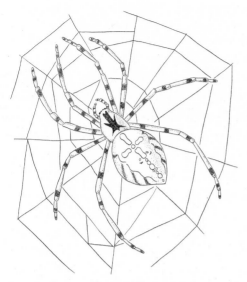

human has ever been killed solely by a spider bite. The creatures just don't pack much venom.

Spiders do dispatch insects, however, and a good thing that is. "Without spiders there would certainly be no people, because they are far away the most abundant predators of insects on the planet," says Crawford. "Without spiders exercising control, the large number of insects that eat plants would go boom and bust like locusts." An orb weaver spider, such as the heroine of *Charlotte's Web*, can catch a hundred insects a day. Her dot-size cousins in forest duff eat one or two. Ecological studies have shown that 40 percent of insects die by being eaten by spiders. One English researcher, William Bristowe, has estimated that the weight of insects consumed annually by spiders in Britain exceeds the combined weight of that nation's human population. Don't like bugs? Then tolerate spiders.

Late summer through early fall is the time of year when spiders intrude on Northwest consciousness. Huge orb webs are lit with dew. Bushes blossom with delicate sheet webs. Creepy house spiders scurry across living rooms. Arachnids the size of a silver dollar can greet us at the sink. Good morning!

Ironically, this is also a time when the overall population of spiders is at low ebb, Crawford explains, because many species have already completed their annual cycle and spiders are extremely intolerant of late-summer drought. Spiders like rain, and it is only the bigger, more obvious species that catch our attention late in the year.

Most native Northwest spiders tend to be small and rather innocuous. The big house spiders are newcomer showoffs that rode in on shipping containers or bunches of food. For example, that companion in your bathtub is probably a European giant house spider that was desperately thirsty, smelled water, and now can't crawl back up the steep porcelain. Contrary to myth, he didn't come up your drain, though spiders washed down a drain can occasionally cling to one side of the pipe and crawl back up later.

That spider hurtling across your living room did not come inside to escape the cold. He's been around your house as egg or youngster the whole time, is finally at sexual maturity, and is risking a rare appearance because of his frantic search for a mate. The poor guy isn't a would-be attacker, he's a sex-crazed, would-be lover. Each whap of your newspaper ends a quest for amour.

It's not true that female spiders, including the black widow, eat their mates (at least not usually), but a spider does have only thirty thousand brain cells, or a million times fewer than we do. "Spiders are little tiny robots," says Crawford, "simpler than a desktop computer." But they are programmed to do a few simple things—like killing whatever hits their nest— very, very well.

Accordingly, a male spider looking for love must do so gingerly. Most spiders, despite boasting six to eight eyes, have such dim eyesight that a female can accidentally turn a suitor into a snack before he has a chance to explain. But spiders also have an acute sense of air and web vibration. As a result, some male spiders do a little dance at the edge of a web to demonstrate their prowess and charm. Others pluck the web strings to make an alluring vibration that gets the female to relax. A few even have to use their silk to tie the object of their affection down until the business is done. After courtship succeeds, the brief adult cycle ends, eggs are laid, the adults die, and the stage is set for spider emergence the following year.

Spiders are in the animal group known as arachnids, which includes scorpions, mites, ticks, and harvestmen, daddy longlegs with a single-sectioned body and no silk or venom. The name comes from the legend of Arachne, who made the mistake of beating the goddess Athena in a weaving contest and was changed into a spider. Arachnids have eight legs; insects have six. Spiders have two body sections; insects have three. Spiders are carnivores; many insects are plant eaters. But spiders do not have a monopoly on silk: three orders of insects, including the moths and butterflies, make silk as well.

Their web-weaving prowess is what makes spiders so fascinating and has earned them a place in human lore as smart, patient, sly, treacherous, bloodthirsty, industrious, and persistent. The Academy Award–winning movie *Braveheart* suggests that the death of William Wallace finally persuaded the vacillating Robert the Bruce to lead the Scots to victory over the English, but Scottish legend insists otherwise. When Bruce was recovering from wounds and defeat, so legend has it, he observed the tireless repair of webs by spiders ("wee beasties") and vowed not to give up.

Even the Itsy Bitsy Spider of nursery fame keeps climbing up that spout.

A spider's abdomen can produce up to six different kinds of silk by ejecting syrupy protein out of little nozzles. The faucets reorient the protein molecules into a solid strand which is only a tenth the diameter of silkworm silk but, for its weight, stronger than steel and more elastic than nylon. The webs of some large African species are so resilient they are hard for humans to push through. New Guinea natives construct bamboo hoops, set the frame in the jungle for giant spiders to build a web on, and then use it to scoop up fish.

Spiders can produce up to a thousand feet of silk at a time, but the line is so thin and light that repeated attempts to commercialize spider silk production have failed. (One problem: getting enough flies for the work force to eat.) Scientists are still trying to synthesize spider silk for industrial use, and the Defense Department thinks a vest of the stuff would stop bullets better than Kevlar.

While a web seems miraculous, spiders have been working on the problem for at least 380 million years. Scientists speculate that the first "webs" were simply trip lines laid by burrowing spiders that then rushed out to seize and kill their prey. Insects may have evolved flight to avoid these tendrils, and spider web-building perhaps then evolved to trap flying bugs. While the geometric orb web catches our eye, spiders also build webs like sheets, three dimensional boxes, ladders, and so on.

Paul Hillyard's *The Book of the Spider* records that one orb web twenty-two inches in diameter required one hundred and twenty-two feet of silk with seven hundred connections, and yet it was completed in only thirty-six minutes. Orb weavers typically rebuild their web each day, sometimes recycling an old one by eating it.

Construction starts when a spider releases a filament to the breeze so it can be wafted across an open space and stick on the opposite side. This initial attachment is rapidly reinforced and the web goes up and down from there, the spider using its leg span to measure out distances between lines. (Spiders launched into space by NASA experienced several days of confusion from weightlessness and then still managed to build webs.) When an insect hits a web, the spider uses venom to paralyze it, ties it down with new line, and either sucks out its liquids or breaks down its flesh by spewing out digestive juices. Spiders don't stick to their own trap because they run on the nonsticky radial strands. They also have an oily coating on their legs.

All very impressive, you're thinking. But if spiders are so swell, why do they haunt literary characters from Little Miss Muffett to the denizens of a Stephen King novel? Why did English schoolchildren pick spiders as the second most-disliked animal (after snakes in one poll, and rats in another) in two separate surveys? There's no question that, with the exception of E. B. White's Charlotte (certainly one of the boldest gambles for a heroine in all publishing), spiders get bad press. They lurk. They snare. They poison. They dissolve their victims. They seem sneaky, swollen, wiggly, and ugly. They're a staple of Halloween.

But Crawford, who has been bitten only twice in a lifetime of handling tens of thousands of spiders, argues that a lot of our fear of spiders is trained, not instinctual. Adults shriek. Siblings squeal. Movies exaggerate. And all the poor spider wants to do is stay out of our way. Spiders will bite as a last resort if threatened or trapped in clothing, but unlike mosquitoes, fleas, and ticks (which bite to get blood nourishment), or bees (which sting to protect nests), spiders have little reason to bite human beings. They can't eat us. Their venom is powerful but too slight to kill us. They can't see, smell, or hear well; they are extremely vulnerable to thirst, and their soft bodies make them prey for a host of creatures. Typical spiders are cowards by necessity. They can sprint for only ten or fifteen seconds before they run out of steam. Of the thirty-four thousand known spider species, only five hundred can deliver even a significant bite to a human.

Crawford and many experts believe spider bites are frequently misdiagnosed, and deaths infrequent to nonexistent. It's true, however, that some spiders can make victims severely sick. Luckily, most dangerous spiders don't live in western Washington and Oregon. There is a false black widow that can be found in Seattle basements, but it's not dangerous. More worrisome is the hobo spider, a 1930s immigrant now found all over the Northwest. Looking much like the common giant house spider we all jump at, the hobo can make victims ill for a week and give them a sore lasting up to six weeks.

Fortunately the giant house spider, an immigrant that entered Seattle about 1960, is the hobo's deadly enemy and is making it increasingly rare. Unfortunately, it can take an expert to tell the two apart, meaning we can easily whack good spiders that are useful sentries against bad.

While encountering a dangerous spider is rare, spiders encounter dangerous humans all the time. Spiders are eaten as satay in Southeast Asia and are gobbled to promote long life in China. Tarantulas are barbecued by Amazonian Indians and their fangs used as toothpicks.

When we're not eating them, however, we can admire them. Spiders are amazing creatures, found three-quarters of the way up Mount Everest and thriving under winter snow-pack in the Pacific Northwest. An underwater spider in Europe constructs a silken diving bell and takes air bubbles down with it as an oxygen supply. The South American goliath tarantula grows to the size of a dinner plate.

Spiders are not just agents of death but also colonizers of life, and what makes *Charlotte's Web* a classic is that it addresses these poles of existence. At the end of the book, Wilbur has been saved, Charlotte will die, and yet her eggs will hatch into young that will balloon away on spider silk. This is not fiction but astonishing fact.

Some young spiders release loops of line snagged by the wind. They've been collected by aircraft as high as fourteen thousand feet and by ships a thousand miles from land. The first animal found on the island devastated by the eruption of Krakatoa was a spider, busily spinning its web.

Ballooning spiders were also early recolonizers of the ashen plains of Mount St. Helens. Researchers found them para-chuting in at the rate of one spider per square meter per day, like commandos on a beachhead.

What is interesting about animals in our Northwest is how they reflect back at us: how much they are like us, or, more accurately, how much we are like them. Spiders are cruel but it is a natural cruelty, and they achieve it by spinning gos-samer objects of resilient delicacy with industry, perseverance, patience, economy, and good timing that gives us—after a morning fog coats their work with diamonds—a much more habitable and glorious world than we would otherwise have.

We do well to manage the same.

THE
CLOCKWORK
WORLD

Geology

THE GROUND IS CRUMBLING BENEATH our feet. It wasn't always so, or so we thought. A few decades ago the Pacific Northwest seemed a fairly safe place to stand. The threat of serious earthquakes was something only Californians lived with. Our volcanoes seemed dormant, our bluffs fine for building homes on, our scenery timeless. Then came a revolution in geologic theory called plate tectonics, the explosion of Mount St. Helens, and field work by geologists that has exposed the cracks in our crust and shattered our complacency like a bull in a china shop. By the beginning of the twenty-first century, "rock solid" has begun to sound as much a Northwest oxymoron as urban "traffic flow."

This change in awareness is a remarkable achievement by geologists who have hiked, climbed, drilled, canoed, dived to the ocean floor, and scrambled around volcanic craters. The rest of us, maybe, are happier not knowing. Still, let us review what the rock hounds have told us:

＊ The Puget Sound basin averages a magnitude 6 or so earthquake about every thirty-five to forty years. Sure enough, a magnitude 6.8 temblor struck the Olympia area on February 28, 2001, some thirty-six years after the last shakeup in 1965.

❋ In the last sixty-two hundred years, there have been thirteen offshore "subduction zone" earthquakes of approximately magnitude 8 or 9, as large as the most powerful quakes on the globe. When the next one hits, shaking will occur for several minutes, coastal areas will be battered with tsunami waves, and damage may stretch from northern California to British Columbia. These earthquakes occur about three to five centuries apart. The last one was approximately three hundred years ago.

❋ Seattle is bisected by a "Seattle Fault" and is underlaid with a weirdly uneven layer of bedrock that is still being mapped and deciphered. If the fault were to move as dramatically as it did a thousand years ago, much of the city could be leveled. The U.S. Geological Survey is working to determine its present-day potential.

❋ Postcard-perfect Mount Rainier has been characterized by geologists as the most hazardous volcano in America, not so much because of its potential for eruption but because so many people live in the probable path of mudflows (lahars) that could slide without warning. One such lahar about fifty-six hundred years ago covered a hundred square miles and buried the present-day sites of Enumclaw, Auburn, and Sumner. A smaller mudflow six centuries back buried the future site of Orting and reached Tacoma. Chance of a repeat in a resident's lifetime? One in seven. Just a minor slide in 1963 spilled fourteen million cubic yards of rock onto Emmons Glacier.

❋ The Puget Sound basin has been in a slump since the last Ice Age as unstable gravel, sand, and clay bluffs periodically erode and slowly refill Puget Sound. The last big mess to topple houses and swallow roads was in 1997. The trigger? Heavy rain.

All this doesn't even consider Mount St. Helens, which lost thirteen hundred feet of elevation when it blew up in 1980, killing fifty-seven people. The volcano built a lava dome in its crater a thousand feet high in just five years and is expected to pop to life again sometime this century. Mount Baker heated ominously in 1975, and both it and Mount Hood occasionally spout steam. It's enough to make a Northwesterner want to move—except for the hurricanes, tornadoes, blizzards, heat waves, floods, fires, erosions, insects, and crime of everywhere else. Besides, it's pretty here—and that's because of geology too.

We owe much of our beauty to the last Ice Age and its bulldozing glaciers. They carved Puget Sound so deeply that there's an underwater canyon not far from the Edmonds ferry dock more than nine hundred feet deep. The ice finished sculpting our mountains and triggered more than forty catastrophic floods across eastern Washington, which in turn

carved the coulees of the "channeled scablands" and dropped boulders far up the Willamette Valley.

This ice acted on a region already upended by plate tectonics. The 200-million-year-long collision between North and South America and the floor of the Pacific Ocean has thrust up mountain ranges from Alaska to Cape Horn, including the Cascades, Olympics, and Oregon Coast Ranges. Our rain, our rivers, our lakes, our forests, our desert, and our farmland all owe their origin to this partnership of fire and ice.

The Northwest has three world-class geologic destinations of stark and eerie beauty that should be on the "must-see" list of any resident. The first, of course, is Mount St. Helens, which is simply the most accessible volcanic, geologic, and biological outdoor laboratory on the planet right now. Go not just for the violence of the blast zone but also for the changes that have followed: the erosion of the mudflows, the new lakes and wetlands, the colonization by plants and animals, and the wonderful wildflowers of midsummer. The volcano is not just visual spectacle. It's a philosophy thesis in ash and rubble, a meditation on permanence, change, decay, renewal, and perspective. Part tragedy and part prayer, it changes with every visit.

The second electrifying feature is Grand Coulee, the basalt canyon that runs south of the dam by the same name and which is the Ice Age bed of the Columbia River. Cliffs remain of an Ice Age waterfall that would have dwarfed any in today's world. The coulee is a dramatic reminder of a cyclic flooding that occurred an estimated forty to two hundred times, when glaciers that dammed a temporary lake repeatedly broke in western Montana. Each time, the ice dams released about five hundred cubic miles of water that roared across the Northwest in a wall up to one thousand feet high and at speeds approaching sixty miles per hour, redrawing the surface of the Columbia Plateau before surging through the Columbia River Gorge and drowning the future sites of Portland and Vancouver. The plateau itself represents one of the greatest lava flows on the planet, covering one hundred thousand square miles.

The third is Crater Lake, the remains of a Rainier-size Mount Mazama that blew itself apart about seven thousand years ago and ejected more than thirty times as much ash into the air as Mount St. Helens did in 1980. The resulting deposits can be found across most of the Northwest. The sapphire blue lake in the crater, hundreds of feet deep, is both stunningly beautiful and a disturbing reminder of periodic cataclysm.

These are simply the headliners of enough geologic melodrama to power a soap opera. "People once thought that West Coast earthquakes would not be major except around the San Andreas Fault," recalls David Hyndman, a geologist at the University of Montana and co-author of a recommended series of roadside guides to our geologic landscape. "Now we know that's not true. The Northwest has the potential for earthquakes as big as anywhere in the world."

Northwest geology is not just dramatic; it's vital in understanding how to live here. Discoveries by scientists are slowly percolating into not just earthquake planning but into building codes, land-use decisions, shoreline management, and environmental policy. Geology is fundamental as well to understanding our environment. Our oceans, our atmosphere, and our climate all ultimately come from rocks. Water and atmospheric gases were excreted by early volcanism at the beginning of our planet and the position of mountain ranges or ocean-blocking landforms such as the Isthmus of Panama dictate climate and much of evolution. One theory is that the joining of North and South America triggered enough climate change in distant Africa to get our ancestors out of the trees and jump-start human evolution.

Because the present position of drifting continents tends to block easy ocean flow between the warm equator and the cold poles, conditions have favored the creation of northern hemisphere Ice Ages for the past two million years. There have been at least five and maybe as many as twenty glaciations which have covered most of British Columbia and northern Washington.

Human civilization has risen in a brief interglacial period of relative warmth that is outside an Ice Age norm. Some eighteen thousand years ago, the Puget Sound basin was buried under ice that was a mile thick at Bellingham, three thousand feet deep at Seattle, and fifteen hundred feet at Olympia. The Cascades and Olympics were dominated by glaciers.

The present interglacial period is well on its way toward ending, with the warmest part of the intermission about five thousand years ago. While human-caused global warming may temporarily interrupt the trend, past patterns would suggest the ice should return sometime in the next ten thousand years.

In the meantime we're enjoying it here, trying to understand risk from infrequent but catastrophic events. In a frenetic world in which computing power has been doubling every eighteen months, geologic time is hard to grasp. We in the Pacific Northwest are at the cutting edge of a planetary drama caused by drifting continents that move about as fast as your fingernails grow. That ponderous motion is quick enough to build mountain ranges, ignite volcanoes, and trigger earthquakes.

Two hundred million years ago a supercontinent that geologists call *Pangaea* broke up and gave birth to the Atlantic Ocean, which has been widening a few inches each year ever since. This widening has sent our side of North America crowding out over the Pacific, curling over the San Juan and Pacific plates of the ocean floor. Yee haw! Unfortunately the ride goes in jerks and jolts, with the Olympics hiccupping upward from time to time and the Cascade volcanoes throwing off some fireworks.

Now, two hundred million years is a long time, pretty much encompassing the age of dinosaurs and mammals. Yet it represents only the last 5 percent of the Earth's much longer history, and much of western Washington and Oregon have been around only for the last one percent of planetary time. Mount St. Helens and the Ice Age floods occupy hardly a blink, and there are Douglas fir trees here that have existed five times longer than Euro-American civilization. Our tenure is incredibly brief, and our ability to comprehend the rhythm of geologic change is limited.

Back when Pangaea broke up, the coastline of North America was roughly at the Washington-Idaho border. What happened next is complicated in its details but simple in summary, which is that, as the continent pushed westward, large islands or *terranes* that were out in the Pacific Ocean bumped up against the shoreline to make up much of the Pacific Northwest.

At that time offshore geology was similar to that observed off Asia today, meaning there were big clumps of land offshore similar to the Japanese islands. The Okanogan Highlands of Washington and British Columbia docked about 175 million years ago. The North Cascades made port about 100 million years back. The San Juans and Vancouver Island tied up shortly after. South of there, however, a huge bay covered much of what would become western Washington and Oregon.

Prehistoric rivers eventually dumped enough sediment to make a flat coastal shoreline of swamps about where Seattle is now. The plants that grew fifty million years ago would eventually become the coal and gas deposits of nearby Black Diamond and Flaming Geyser State Park.

This flat landscape began to change when the central and southern Cascades started rising about forty million years ago, the Columbia River cutting downward as fast as the mountains rose to create its present gorge. Magma boiled out of the ocean floor, hardened, and was scraped off by the collision of the plates to start piling up the eastern and central Olympics about thirty-five million years ago, which explains why a mountain range with no volcanoes has so much volcanic rock: it originated at the bottom of the sea.

About seventeen million years ago the Cascade volcanoes snuffed out and vast new lava flows rolled out from the Idaho border. One theory is that an asteroid crash in eastern Oregon triggered the sudden change. Then things shifted west again, the Cascades began to grow once more, and the Olympics piled higher.

Curiously stuck between the two ranges was that flat, ancient bayshore area that extended from Vancouver, British Columbia, to the southern end of Oregon's Willamette Valley. As erosion of the new mountains continued, the basin began to fill in, creating the relatively flat land where the majority of Northwesterners live today.

Details are not easy to discern. Most of the Puget Sound basin is covered by gravel and water left by past Ice Ages, meaning that in Seattle most of the original bedrock and sediments are buried under hundreds of feet of glacial debris. Four vast glaciations have been identified and named but there may have been many more, each new one erasing much of the evidence of the one before. The most recent glacier finished digging Puget Sound and laid down the north-south glacial ridges, called *drumlins*, that many people live on. Seattle's Capitol and Beacon Hills are a drumlin, artificially cut in two by excavation for Interstate 90.

At the height of the Ice Age the ice was so heavy that almost all of the heavily populated area of the Puget Sound basin was pressed beneath present-day sea level. As the ice retreated, the land rebounded upward. As the glaciers melted, global sea level rose as well by an estimated four hundred feet, the rising land and the rising sea causing a complicated dance of changes resulting in our final topography. Much of Washington's Kitsap Peninsula, for example, was for a while an archipelago of islands in a glacial lake.

The ice excavation of Puget Sound seems unbelievable until you remember that this natural bulldozer was up to a mile high. It left Seattle's Lake Washington so deep—two hundred feet in places—that commuters must rely on floating bridges. Elliott Bay is three hundred feet deep on average, and up to eighty feet deep near many shorelines. In many places the central Sound is so deep that light doesn't penetrate. Yet the Sound undulates between deep basins and high sills: its entrance at Admiralty Inlet is only about two hundred and fifteen feet deep and the sill in the Tacoma Narrows is just one hundred and fifty feet.

This same unevenness is seen above the water, of course,

where steep topography produces splendid views and not-so-splendid traffic and engineering challenges. While the glacial leftovers called *till* make pretty good underpinnings for buildings, till slowly erodes where cut by saltwater waves or river erosion. Bluffs at Discovery Park in Seattle are estimated to retreat at a rate of eighty feet per century. The joint between Ice Age layers of sand and clay can slip in heavy rainstorms, triggering disastrous slides.

In short, the Puget Sound basin is literally going downhill and could fill Puget Sound in a mere ten million years—except that new glaciers will probably re-dig the waterway many times long before then. Volcanoes will explode, earthquakes rumble, landslides tumble, rivers flood. We live on one of the most plastic places on the planet, constantly resculpted. As worrisome as this can be at times, it's also wonderful. The tumult makes the Pacific Northwest not only beautiful but thought provoking. Looking at the ground is like looking at the stars: it puts things in perspective.

You can stride across old ocean magma that boiled out a hundred million years ago in the San Juan Islands. Nearby, on Whidbey Island, you can sift through glacial rocks left behind just fifteen thousand years ago. You can find traces of the ash left by Mount Mazama almost seven thousand years ago and road shoulder dustings from St. Helens still in living memory. You can poke at coal from prehistoric swamps in King County and, near Vantage, Washington, you can look at the petrified trunks of a forest entombed by lava. At Washington's Willapa Bay you can see the trunks of a ghost forest killed by a tsunami wave during an earthquake that probably occurred on January 17, 1700.

Our Northwest is as littered with monuments as Europe,

but ours are of geologic history, not human history. We live in a place both unimaginably old and disturbingly young. If culture is influenced by landscape, then maybe our rocks have helped produce our curious blend of the conservative and innovative, the cautious and the bold: a Northwest society on the very edge of continental and technological change.

Tides

IT IS PHENOMENON ENOUGH TO POWER A disaster movie, an apocalyptic nightmare. Imagine an ocean wave reaching halfway around the world. Imagine an onrushing swell that pushes twenty to thirty cubic kilometers of water through the Strait of Juan de Fuca and mercilessly churns the Northwest's inland sea, flooding a hundred square miles of shorelands. It could happen. In fact, it *does* happen. Twice a day this flood pours in, a quarter of its flow turning into Puget Sound and three-quarters pouring north through the San Juans and along the east side of Vancouver Island.

The flood is called the tide, and its cyclic circulation sustains the fecund biology of what University of Washington oceanographer Richard Strickland calls, in his book on Puget Sound, *The Fertile Fjord.* The tide influences the flow of marine traffic, with everything from sailboats to supertankers preferring to catch a favorable flow. It dictates how easily we can get rid of sewage, and where sewage plants and outfalls should go. It sustains a rich intertidal zone of life which may have been the path that animals took eons ago to get from the sea to the land.

Moreover, the Pacific Northwest's peculiar geography produces some of the strongest tidal currents in the world. Currents can reach as fast as six knots in the Tacoma Narrows, nine knots at Deception Pass between Whidbey and Fidalgo Islands, and up to sixteen knots, or nearly twenty miles per hour, in several narrows in British Columbia.

Curt Ebbesmeyer, an oceanographer at Evans-Hamilton, Inc., in Seattle, has put out fifty thousand small wooden cards in local waters to track our complex currents, so that local governments can predict where treated and untreated sewage will go. He found that half of those dropped near Victoria's untreated sewage eventually wound up in Puget Sound, somewhat sullying international relations.

As an example of tidal power he cites the floating journey of a corpse. A man jumped from the Tacoma Narrows Bridge around three A.M. on February 5, 1988, dying on impact. The body fetched up a day and a half later, twenty miles away at Alki Point in Seattle. Investigators calculated that the jumper had first drifted south several miles to Fox Island (where a floating cadaver was spotted by a fisherman), and then reversed and floated north through Colvos Passage on the west side of Vashon Island before swinging east to Seattle. Because of the pumping bellows of the Narrows, tidal currents always flow clockwise, going north on the west side of Vashon and south on the east. Mariners have taken advantage of this trick since aboriginal times.

Literally billions of dollars in public spending ride on our tides. At Admiralty Inlet, at the mouth of Puget Sound, about one-third of the water exits to the Strait of Juan de Fuca during each tidal cycle, and two-thirds is sucked back under in a revolving pattern. It takes about three tidal cycles for an aver-

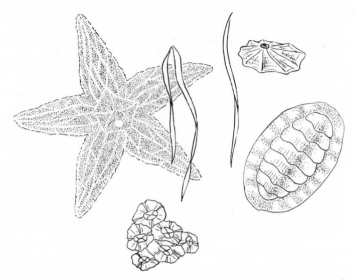

age molecule of pollution to head toward the diffuse ocean. Deeper in the Sound, the same cleansing action may require thirty to sixty tidal cycles.

Citing such numbers, scientists have hotly disagreed whether Puget Sound is half clean or half dirty. Some argued the tides flush so efficiently that Seattle's West Point sewage treatment plant needed only primary treatment instead of the much more expensive secondary cleansing, but the Environmental Protection Agency ultimately disagreed. The region's Renton treatment plant's pipe was rerouted to take advantage of dispersing tides to keep pollutants out of Elliott Bay.

Tides are also a window into the workings of the universe. Aside from apples bonking him on the head, tides were some of the most compelling evidence to Sir Isaac Newton that gravity exists not just on earth but in the attraction between astronomical bodies. Earth's tides are primarily caused by the pull of the moon and sun. The bulge of water averages about three feet high in midocean and then is exaggerated when it hits shore, owing to narrowing sounds and bays.

Accurately predicting tides is one of the most complex problems in the natural world. While astronomical influences can be precisely forecast, the wind, the atmospheric pressure, and the piling up of ocean water during El Niño periods means a tide forecast can routinely be off a foot or two, explains Harold Mofjeld, the tidal expert at the National Oceanographic and Atmospheric Administration's Pacific Marine Lab in Seattle. Laymen, however, can keep in mind a few basic principles for boating, clam digging, beachcombing, and sand-castle building:

❀ Northwest waters have one extreme high and low tide per day, coupled with a more moderate high and low. This is just one of several tidal patterns observed around the world.

❀ Each day's high and low lags behind the previous day's by about fifty minutes. This is because the lunar day of moonrises and moonsets exceeds the solar day by 50.47 minutes. The moon rotates around the Earth in the same direction the Earth is rotating on its axis, but it steadily falls behind, like a dog chasing a car. The ratio between the solar and lunar days is also slowly changing. Friction caused by the tides is helping to slow the rotation of the Earth by two-tenths of a second every thousand years, meaning that early in its history, Earth's day was only six hours long.

❀ Tides are most extreme each month at the new and full moons, and least extreme at the half moon. Reason? At a full moon, the Earth is between the moon and sun, and at a new moon, the moon is between Earth and sun; in both cases, moon and sun are combining to pull in the same direction, mounding up a particularly high wave of water that causes the tide. At a half moon, the moon's pull is at a ninety-degree angle to that of the sun, lessening the bulge. The big tides are called "spring" tides, not because of the season but from springing, or lively, water. The small tides are called "neap" from the Anglo-Saxon *nep*, meaning scant, or lacking.

❀ The year's biggest tides are always near the summer and winter solstice, or June 21 and December 21. In summer, the super-low tide occurs in the daytime; in winter, at night. The same orbital tilt that produces summer and winter as the Earth circles the sun, also produces times of maximum solar pull on our oceans. The complex tidal cycle can throw the actual date of the biggest tides some one to two weeks off the actual solstice.

❀ Tides tend to be more extreme at Olympia at the end of Puget Sound (with a range averaging 14.4 feet), and less at its entrance, at Port Townsend (where the range averages 8.3 feet). Olympia lags an hour and a half and Shelton about two hours behind Port Townsend in the time of high and low tides, because it takes that much longer for the tidal wave to reach them. Similarly, tides tend to be greater at the northern end of the Strait of Georgia, near Campbell River and Desolation Sound, than at Victoria. It's like water sloshing back and forth in a bathtub: the wave crests highest at either end.

❀ American tide tables and navigation charts average the lowest low tide (meaning the day's more extreme low tide) over many years to get an average "zero." Since some tides must be below any average, this means many days have a minus tide where water can be shallower than what the chart says. Americans use *feet* and *fathoms*, a fathom being six feet. Canadians more sensibly use the lowest tide ever as their zero point—meaning Canada doesn't have minus tides. Canadians use *meters*. Ignore the international difference, and your boat may go crunch.

NOAA "does try to err on the side of safety," Mofjeld notes. In a sampling of soundings of a harbor's bottom, for example, chart-makers will pick the shallowest to give fair warning.

There, you're an expert. Or are you?

Understanding tides in detail is one of the most devilishly complex problems in science. Not just sun and moon but wind, the configuration of the bottom, the position of land masses, the rotation of the Earth, barometric pressure, temperature, and a host of other variables—at least thirty-seven, according to textbooks—influence the tides and their accompanying currents.

Warm water expands more than cold water, changing sea level. High pressure squeezes the ocean down, while extreme low pressure—during a hurricane, for example—allows it to swell up. Wind can join with a tidal current to mound even more water against the shore, or can fight it.

Big tides funneled into a small area—such as at Canada's Bay of Fundy or Alaska's Turnagain Arm—can produce stupendous tides. Several years ago a woman was drowned near Anchorage when she drove onto the mud of Turnagain Arm, became stuck, and then sank into the mud herself while trying to push her vehicle. Before she could be freed, the tide returned.

Tide records have been kept in Seattle since 1899. A gauge at the downtown ferry dock bounces sound pulses off the top of water rising and falling in a tube. Its data is constantly being fed to the Tidal Analysis Branch of NOAA in Washington, D.C. Super-computers crunch the data, trying to come up with ever more precise predictions.

Because the sun-Earth-moon system takes 18.6 years to go through the cycle of variations of their positions to one another, records must be kept at least that long in any bay to make near-accurate predictions. Even that length of time is an approximation: it actually takes 20,940 years for every possible astronomical variation to play out.

The primary cause of the tide is fairly simple. The gravity of the sun and moon pull the ocean toward them, creating a standing bulge or wave. As the Earth rotates under this wave, the tide moves around the world. At its simplest, this would produce one high tide and one low per day.

In actual fact there are two bulges, the second directly opposite the gravitational bulge. As an analogy, oceanographer Strickland suggests imagining the Earth and moon as two dancers with arms locked, twirling in a circle. One wave is towards the moon, and the opposite is caused by a kind of centrifugal force, as if the cape or dress of a dancer was flying out as they twirled. That flying cape is the second wave. Thus the Earth is rotating under two waves, producing two high tides and two lows per day.

Unfortunately, the only place in which the ocean is open enough for a model this simple to really work is the Southern Ocean that circles around Antarctica, unblocked by land. Everywhere else the waves are being struck by continents as the Earth turns.

The resultant sloshing is maddeningly complex. The bounce of the tides sets up a kind of resonance that can reinforce or cancel tides. In the Gulf of Mexico, for example, the undulation works to cancel out a second tide, producing just one high and one low per day. Here in the Northwest, it means our tides are uneven.

Where land masses squeeze together, tides can be accen-

tuated. They tend to be greater in the North Pacific, where
North America and Siberia lean toward each other, than at
the equator.

The Earth's rotation also produces a swirling motion
called the Coriolis Force which sets up that pinwheeling look
of atmospheric storms and hurricanes. It also gives north-south
direction to the primarily east-west tides. As a result, tides on
our coast tend to march north, cresting in California first, then
Washington, and eventually Alaska.

The prevailing winds that tend to mound waters up at one
side of the Pacific or the other during La Niña and El Niño
also modify sea level and resulting tide levels.

Winter storms with low barometric pressure and high
winds can push water against a Puget Sound shoreline at high
tide, creating big waves and damage.

And so on and so on.

Tides are essential, Strickland notes. Puget Sound supports three times as much plankton, the base of the food chain,
as does Washington's coast. It supports ten times as much as
the deep ocean. The reason for this is tidal mixing that brings
nutrients from deep water up to feed the tiny creatures. The
tides also pump oxygen into Puget Sound basins that would
otherwise become dead seas.

A sailboat or kayak going from Seattle to the San Juans
can cut its travel time by more than half by paying close attention to tidal currents. Cruise ships departing Vancouver for
Alaska will often leave within an hour of each other to catch
favorable tides through narrow passes. Tugs with heavy tows
will often wait in a quiet bay for six hours to catch a favorable tide.

In British Columbia the issue is one of life or death,
because fierce tidal currents can turn rocks into severe nav-

igational hazards. Seymour Narrows, at the southern end of the main shipping lanes up the Inside Passage, had sunk or severely damaged fourteen major ships and one hundred smaller vessels and had killed one hundred and fourteen people by 1958. Then a $3 million engineering effort tunneled under midchannel Ripple Rock and packed it with thirteen hundred tons of explosives, producing the biggest non-nuclear peacetime explosion in the world.

One reason swift tidal currents are so terrifying is that the kinetic energy of water is proportional to the square of its velocity. This means a ten-knot current has four times the energy of one of five knots, and a fifteen-knot current has nine times the energy. British Columbia currents can be so strong that they are safely navigated only in slack water. At full flood they can produce whirlpools that are two or three feet deeper than surrounding water and "overfalls," or standing waves, that are two or three feet high.

Mysterious to any mariner is the observation that slack water does not necessarily occur at the time of high or low tide. Incoming flood currents, for example, can run an hour or two past the high in some places. Why doesn't the current more quickly reverse? Strickland explains that the lag occurs when the tide gets hung up in a narrow passage and the uphill side hasn't finished flowing to fill in the downhill side, even when the tide everywhere else is turning.

Also odd is when the flood or incoming tide is always greater than the ebb, or vice versa. This can occur when tidal flows tend to round an island in a consistent direction. At Anacortes's Guemes Channel, for example, water tends to flow clockwise around Guemes Island, making the channel's outgoing ebb flow consistently greater than its flood.

Rivers, of course, can also create an imbalance. The fresh

water of the Fraser River at Vancouver tends to "entrain," or pull, salt water as it pours out, snowballing into a volume up to ten times that of the river itself and creating a strong seaward current that can be measured all the way to the Pacific Ocean. At the mouth of the Strait of Juan de Fuca, the water volume can reach one hundred and fifty thousand cubic meters per second.

Because the mix of fresh and salt water is lighter, this outflow occurs on the surface. Underneath, to make up for the loss of water, is an inflow of saltier currents from the ocean. Because of Coriolis Force rotation, incoming currents tend to be stronger on the Olympic Peninsula side of the Strait of Juan de Fuca and outgoing currents stronger on the Vancouver Island side.

Tidal patterns, coupled with wind, are critical to forecasting wave conditions at the entrance of the Columbia River. An incoming tide and outgoing current can cause huge breakers in a storm, while tide and river current in sync can make the water lie flat.

Tidal currents themselves can be thought of as a series of rivers, flowing back and forth through the channels between islands and headlands. When these rivers meet at the end of a point they bounce, swirl, dive, and boil, creating tide rips that can greatly exaggerate wind-generated waves and provide rich feeding grounds for sea life. The intertidal zone between sea and land is similarly bountiful in life as plants and animals take advantage of tide movement that brings in food and nutrients.

What this means, of course, is that our twice-daily disaster movie of incoming tidal water is not a disaster at all. Rather it is the astronomical pump that flushes our bays and estuaries clean, infuses our water with nutrients, makes an intricate mosaic of our currents, and creates the mudflats, saltwater marshes, and seaweed-strewn rocky shores that teem with life.

What if the moon didn't exist? Without the moon our tides would be much smaller, and our Northwest would not be the Northwest we know but rather a more sterile place of stagnant, polluted water. Without the moon, the smaller tide might never have encouraged the transition of life from sea to land, and our landscape might be as barren as that white satellite overhead.

Weather

NORTHWEST WEATHER IS LIKE SEX. IT'S mostly in your head. Oh sure, there's a certain amount of shivering and panting that goes with both subjects. Once in a while each rears up to smack you in the side of the head. Mostly, though, your mood depends on your mind. We Northwesterners sing in our rain, or we eye that infrequent yellow orb called the sun with neurotic distrust, expecting it to disappear at any moment. We're disquieted when it doesn't.

"It hasn't rained in three days," a true webfoot trembles. "Is Judgment at hand?"

It's not easy to think about Northwest weather, because agreeing on its essence is like bagging fog. All of the following is arguably true:

❀ We barely have weather, compared to the tornado-blizzard-hurricane-plagued regions of the less fortunate. And we have more weather, in less space and less time, than just about any place in the nation. To demonstrate, drive from wet Forks, to rain-shadow Sequim, to moderate Seattle, to lofty Snoqualmie Pass, to dry Yakima.

❀ Northwest weather is heavenly (moderate) and hellish (dark and clammy).

❀ It's easy to forecast weather here (more of the same, for the next six months), and incredibly difficult, with storms bouncing off mountains and skipping across salt water like Mad Hatter billiards, creating a thousand microclimates that defy easy summary.

❀ It rains a lot (cloudy drizzle) and it doesn't (in inches, in Seattle proper).

❀ We get more snow (Mount Baker set a world record in 1998–1999, at ninety-five *feet*) and less real winter (again, Seattle proper) than any American place at our latitude.

Northwest weather, in other words, is a Zen koan, a riddle you have to answer yourself. You fight it or embrace it.

"Rain is our regional mascot," says Seattle's David Laskin, author of *Rains All the Time*, a layman's bible of local weather lore. But just why this is—one of the points of his book is that it *doesn't* rain all the time, and that in fact our summer droughts are as peculiar as our winter deluges—fascinates him. His theory is that it is the *length* of our wet periods— the fact we have a rainy season—that stamps it in our consciousness. "If you first move here during a long rainy spell, you never really get over it."

November is our month of weather despair. It's not just that it's awful, but that it's going to stay awful until, oh . . . next Fourth of July. Or throughout the next two decades, if atmospheric scientists are right.

If you moved to the Pacific Northwest after 1976, you enjoyed a weather fantasy that only since 1998 has been breaking down toward the dreariness for which we're famous. For fifteen of the eighteen years up until 1994 the region was drier than normal. What has followed since has been dramatic yo-yo swings between wet winters and drought with a trend toward more gloom. University of Washington scientist Nick Mantua thinks the region might have started a cyclic wet period, called Pacific Decadal Oscillation, that could easily linger until 2015, maybe longer. The same soppiness extended from 1947 to 1976.

This would be good for salmon, trees, irrigation, skiing, power companies (each inch of rain on the upper Skagit earns Seattle City Light a million dollars in power sales), and maybe even sex. It would be bad for mental equilibrium if that record snow winter—the wettest in one hundred and five years, according to the National Weather Service—becomes the norm.

Just in time to erase any certainty came a renewed dry spell in the winter of 2000–2001. Some scientists don't believe the oscillation theory at all, of course. And no matter what your point of view, you're almost certain to be half right.

Now, there are two kinds of people in the Pacific Northwest. One is the type who regards the latest deluge or drought with grim horror and is rending his or her garments in anguished betrayal. "What's going on," they want to know, "with the weather!"

The other type has hung around long enough to know that the weather is basically unknowable, mostly boring, and roughly predictable in a general sense. "*What* weather?" they reply.

Growing up in this moderation can make you a little weather dim. It's interesting that many of the authors who have written most eloquently about Northwest gunk and gloom have tended to be from elsewhere: Tom Robbins and Annie Dillard from Virginia, Barry Lopez from New York,

David Wagoner from Indiana, and David Laskin from New Jersey.

But if Nick Mantua is right and we're oscillating between sunny Dr. Jekyll and rainy Mr. Hyde, then it's necessary for us all to decide just how to think about Northwest weather.

A revolution has occurred in the tools available: satellites, Doppler radar, buoys that measure equatorial ocean temperatures, high-speed computers.

Taxpayers have spent $4.5 billion on this gear and as a result, says the National Weather Service, forecasts are "twice as accurate" for those made two to four days in advance. "We have so much weather information now that our problem is condensing it" into a brief forecast, says Bruce Renneke, who's been wrestling with predictions here since 1967.

Two decades ago scientists were unaware of the natural cycles that dictate our weather. Now they boldly forecast entire seasons, with somewhat questionable results. The Weather Service is trying seriously what once only the *Farmer's Almanac* dared.

"This ability is phenomenally exciting," says University of Washington atmospheric scientist Cliff Mass. Even regular forecast computer models now extend out to fifteen days.

And where is the limit? In addition to the El Niño–La Niña cycle, we have the newly discovered Pacific oscillations with their companion Arctic oscillation, proposed by University of Washington atmospheric scientists such as Mike Wallace to explain abnormally warm temperatures in polar regions.

The sun and Earth have orbital cycles of 23,000 years, 41,000 years, 100,000 and 400,000 years that shift climate cards. Human civilization has arisen during an interglacial recess in what has been three million years of Ice Age norm.

Then there's human-caused global warming. There's no question we're causing a dramatic spike in greenhouse gases. There's strong evidence that average temperatures have climbed about a degree the past century. Globally, the warmest years on record have been the past two decades. Our Northwest has seen a spate of record-breaking wet and dry spells in that period. While debate and uncertainty continue, the scientific consensus is that the planet will heat up in the coming century, possibly increasing drought, flood, and the violence of hurricanes.

It will later probably ice up, somewhere in the next several thousand years, as the next Ice Age returns. Scientists have discovered two spooky things by drilling ice cores, studying sea floor sediments, and hunting rocks. One is that our planet's climate has shifted dramatically and quickly many times in the past. The Vikings settled Greenland in a warm spell, and left in a "Little Ice Age" that ran until the early 1800s and regularly froze London's Thames. The second is that our climate, despite such wiggles, has generally been eerily stable for the past ten thousand years, a run of luck we call "normal."

What if it's not?

The good news is that life is short and you'll probably drop dead before any serious future nastiness occurs. For example, a recently forecast sea level rise of twenty feet, occurring if the West Antarctic ice sheet continues its present melting, is supposed to take seven hundred years to complete. Moreover, global warming might actually cause more rain and snow, not less, in the Pacific Northwest: warmer skies hold more water, and some computer models predict it could get dumped here. Oh boy.

But none of this climate stuff tells us much about tomorrow's weather. As Cliff Mass explains, "average" weather on a chart is actually abnormal as experienced day to day: statistically, we're more likely to be above or below any temperature or rainfall mean. We'll still get scorchers in a cool spell and floods in a dry period.

Mentally, you either take delight in such changes or allow yourself to be trapped by them. It all depends on how you approach our weather. We all know it doesn't rain as much, inch for inch, in Seattle as in many other American cities. (Try telling that one in the suburbs of the Cascades foothills, where it pours.) We also know our marine climate produces an unusual late-summer drought and an ungodly number of overcast days.

But explaining Northwest weather isn't just numbers, it's feel. Seattle is as far north as northern Maine, and Bellingham has the same latitude as Newfoundland. On December 21, we get just half the hours of daylight we enjoy on June 21. Add in that gray mattress we call overcast and it can take three winter days to give you the psychological light-fix of one summer day. Rain or no rain, those who can will flee south.

We Northwesterners also, new arrivals contend, have feeble seasons, slush for snow, flat skies, damp cold, and more power outages (thanks to all the tree limbs) than outer Kurdistan. Why, oh why, does anyone move here?

Because it's moderate, thanks to that fifty-degree bathtub next door called the North Pacific. Neither cold snap nor heat wave lingers long because the ocean temperature is always knock-knock-knocking on our doors. Even Portland is generally about five to seven degrees colder in winter and warmer in summer than Seattle, simply because it doesn't have Puget Sound as a giant temperature regulator. At my coastal house, there's often not much more than ten degrees difference between a summer and winter morning. This is not the stuff of high drama.

Moreover, most of us live in a rain shadow that filters out the worst of the wet stuff: it rains four times as much in the western Olympics as in Seattle. In fact, if you go hour by hour, it only rains in Seattle about 11 percent of the time, and just 3 percent of the time in summer, according to calculations made in 1974 by University of Washington atmospheric scientist Phil Church. That means that except for the rare wind or snowstorm, weather isn't much of a limiting factor. If you can put a jacket on and off, you can do most anything, anytime. Moreover, you can drive to a rain forest, snow bank, or sage desert in a few hours.

And if you can endure until summer, it's heaven: low humidity, robin-egg sky, and fresh north breeze. Remember the drought years of the early 1990s? It's not uncommon to go a month without rain, which is a pattern easterners find downright annoying. Nine months of murk and *still* they have to water the grass?

Here are some basic rules about Northwest weather:

✿ Any extremes will disappear in hours or days. Bad weather visits, but it doesn't set up house. Same with a heat wave.

✿ Oregon's Willamette Valley has a reasonable summer, but in the Puget Sound basin the season often doesn't begin until after the Fourth of July, when a blocking high settles over British Columbia. Before then, the warming desert of eastern Washington pulls marine clouds over western Washington. Deal with it.

✿ September can often be the most delightful month.

✿ Statistically, December is wettest, darkest, awfullest.

❀ Your power is going to go out.

❀ February and May offer some nice weather breaks.

❀ March is a blustery, miserable disappointment.

❀ Statistically, late July is the least likely time for rain.

❀ A north wind generally signifies clear weather, while south brings rain. Warm southern winds in winter are the most dangerous flood threat, because they can pack a lot of rain and melt snowpack.

❀ Escape is possible. It can be pouring in the rain cloud "convergence zone" of north Seattle's suburbs but sunny in the rain-shadowed Friday Harbor, chilly in Bellingham but hot in Portland, soaking in Quilleute but parched in Yakima.

So, how to cope? It would help immensely if we weren't so tyrannized by the calendar and the clock. Our infrequent snows should signal a holiday. Instead we make them a disaster by leaping into our cars to cling to schedule. Stay home.

Work a bit of those endless winter evenings to clear your conscience for a mind-clearing walk or paddle during midday. It counters depression.

It's politically incorrect to whine about Northwest weather. Drenching rains are uncommon. Snow is brief. Cold is mild. Humidity is rare. No one feels sorry for you.

On the other hand, it's kind of silly to gush about it. This isn't Hawaii, people. Fog poetry takes you only so far, and then hypothermia sets in. In midwinter, the darkness sucks at the soul. Too much cheeriness and you run the risk of being lynched.

No, you have to *be* the weather in all its boring, bracing drabness. It's this Northwest Zen thing. I can't remember ever hearing much weather-whining from our true natives. Instead the Indians are *like* the weather: people of the gentle handshake, the quiet voice, the thoughtful pause. Polite yet resilient, moderate, patient. Like our skies. To them the weather just . . . is.

So. Ski. Steelhead fish. Sail. Sniff. Squint. Breathe the rain. Be one with the murk.

At the dawn of the twenty-first century the urban Northwest seemed a very un-Northwest place with its big money and brashness and mania for change: L.A. in a palette of grays. It's been another boom time, reminiscent of the booms in gold and timber and fish and war.

If we could organize or corral or schedule the weather, you bet we would.

But we can't, thank goodness, and that may be a saving grace. We need a good wet oscillation to calm us down periodically, cool us off, and soak us through with the environment we've adopted. Northwest weather keeps the lid on, puts things in perspective, reassures us with its dependable dreariness.

It's like wine, candlelight, and seductive clothing. Get in the mood. Button up, go out in the drizzle, smell the sea, and merge. Revel in November.

If you get your mind around it the right way, it can be the best weather you've ever had.

Snow

EACH WINTER THE PACIFIC NORTHWEST is showered with pennies from heaven. Downy flakes and champagne powder if you like snow, mashed potatoes and Cascade crud if you don't.

The white stuff represents food, electricity, recreation, and future stream habitat. "Snow is our white gold," says Philip Mote, a researcher with the Climate Impacts Group at the University of Washington.

He estimates that the Northwest snowpack's value as hydropower and irrigation water is in the billions of dollars, given that a 1994 snow drought cost Yakima Valley farmers alone an estimated $140 million. An absence of white stuff in 2001 helped send power rates soaring and farmers dancing with disaster.

Snow is critical because it doesn't run away. Columbia Basin dam reservoirs have the capacity to capture only about a quarter of annual precipitation, which means that three-quarters of the basin's summer storage depends on the natural white blanket that coats Northwest mountains.

In a wet year, we sell our snow, in the form of electricity, to California. In a dry year, we buy from California's coal, oil, and nuclear plants, and pay dearly.

Let it snow, let it snow, let it snow.

So here's the problem. University of Washington scientists have given a disquieting message to eastern Washington farmers: If current global warming projections are correct, much of our snowpack could be gone within fifty years. Each one degree rise in temperature raises the snow level about three hundred feet, Mote says, and researchers expect a five-degree rise by 2050, which would be enough to eliminate much of our snow-bearing slopes.

"We simply cannot build enough dams in the next few decades to make up for the projected loss of snowpack," he warns.

As Joni Mitchell sings it, you don't know what you've got until it's gone.

The urban Northwest, of course, has a love-hate relationship with snow. It's fine if it stays in its place, like a distant watershed or ski slope. It's nasty when tropical rain front and Arctic cold collide to dump snow on our cities, which are so ill prepared for a snowstorm that a good dump is like pouring syrup onto a computer keyboard.

Urban snow is almost always slippery here because it's so wet. Our terrain is steep, our removal equipment feeble, and our habits so ingrained that we won't take a day off or even slow down. Most urban adults dread snow as earnestly as children long for it.

It wasn't always so. George Washington University historian Bernard Mergen, author of *Snow in America,* traces the seismic shift in American attitudes toward snow to the invention of the automobile. Once upon a time there was a communal attitude of snugness and rest toward snow that was immortalized in Currier and Ives prints of rural New England. When roads were mostly dirt, frost and snow turned an autumn bog into a hard, smooth highway for horses and sleds. Skates and skis provided free recreation. Snow's whiteness illuminated a dark winter landscape.

The car changed that. "Snow was redefined as refuse," Mergen writes, "to be removed as quickly and efficiently as possible." City politicians risked losing their jobs over inept snow plowing. Huge quantities of salt and sand were dumped on thousands of square miles of pavement, contaminating the environment and corroding cars. Studded tires brutalized roadways. Snow changed from beautiful respite to urban hazard, from joy to foe.

The first rotary snowplow appeared in 1884 to help clear train tracks, and highway snowplows followed. Since 1871 there have been more than a hundred patents for snow shovels, with one humorist observing in 1911 that "a snow shovel will find the boundary line between two lots more accurately than the best surveyor."

Now, if tailpipe emissions are truly changing the climate, the automobile may get rid of snow entirely. There's some indication that Northwest snow is already in decline. Seattle's bad winters don't set a particular pattern, having occurred in 1861–62, 1916, 1950, 1968–69, and 1996–97, to name periods *2004* of particularly heavy snow and/or bitter cold. But despite periodic snowy spells, Cascade and Olympic glaciers have been mostly in retreat the past century. Jon Riedel, a National Park Service geologist studying glaciers in the North Cascades, calculates that they've advanced for only about twenty of the last one hundred years, declining the rest of the time.

Some have started advancing again just since 1998, due to good snowpack years, but Riedel projects the long-range pattern will be continued shrinkage. This could cause future problems for fish because glaciers provide most of their meltwater after the snowpack has been exhausted, keeping streams full in the crucial late-summer months.

Glaciers grow when winter snowfall exceeds summer melt and decline when the opposite occurs. While Washington is the most heavily glaciated of the contiguous forty-eight states, once-famous features such as the Paradise Ice Caves on Mount Rainier have simply disappeared.

Keeping count of snow is so important to our economy that it's become a basic job for government. The federal Natural Resources Conservation Service is an agency that operates fifty-four automated climate stations to measure snowpack, and one hundred manual stations, in Washington State alone. Falling snow squeezes a "snow pillow" filled with antifreeze that pushes against a transducer, giving automatic readings of snow weight.

Weight is more revealing than depth. "It's a common fallacy that a foot of snow equals an inch of water," snow quantifier Scott Pattee says. Northwest snow often contains much more. In western Washington the water depth in the snowpack can equal 30 to 50 percent of the snow depth. "That's why skiers call it Cascade concrete."

Linguists debate the number of words that Eskimos have for snow because their language structure allows an incalculable variety, but they're not alone in their descriptive powers. The English language is equally inventive. One survey found at least seventy skier words and terms to describe the white stuff: sugar snow, packed powder, death cookies, and so on. Scientists have even more, listing twenty-eight terms for falling snow and eighty for snow already fallen.

The reason is that frozen water comes in many forms. It was Wilson Alwyn Bentley, a Vermont farmer, who made thousands of photographs of snowflakes between 1884 and 1931 and popularized the idea that no two snowflakes are alike. This is one of those "facts" that is a combination of scientific truth and fanciful poetry; on the one hand, each flake's journey is so individual that it does crystallize in a singular fashion, but on the other hand there are an awful lot of snowflakes, plus an unclear definition of "alike" and no chance of really comparing them all.

So you can swear by the statement or scoff at it.

Rain and snow droplets form around tiny bits of matter suspended in the atmosphere, such as dust, pollutants, bacteria, fungi, and protozoa. As water vapor begins to freeze around these bits of floating grit, it crystallizes according to temperature: hexagonal plates near freezing, then needles as the air is colder, then hollow prismatic columns, back to plates, and so on. They melt, refreeze, collide, break, and reform.

A snowflake can spend from a few minutes to several hours in the air, falling at an average rate of about one foot per second. Because each flake takes a unique path through temperature, wind, and moisture, each tends to crystallize differently by the time it reaches the ground.

Once fallen, snow crystals tend to combine, melt, reform, and squeeze, steadily evolving toward dense snow, then ice, and—in places like Antarctica and Greenland, where snow accumulates to depths of well over a mile—into ice squeezed so free of air bubbles that it becomes clearer than glass. Water molecules tend to absorb all colors except blue, giving snow its ethereal hues at depth.

This continual evolution of snow makes it dangerous. Avalanches are generally triggered by the sliding of a fresh snow across the icy surface of older snow underneath, and making predictions to warn motorists and skiers is dead-serious business. Heavy snow, rain, and wind on an older, rimed snowpack is an invitation to disaster.

Avalanches usually kill several people per year in the Pacific Northwest. In 1910 a slide caused one of the greatest natural disasters in Washington State history when two trains stranded in Stevens Pass were knocked into a canyon by an avalanche on March 1, killing ninety-six.

About 90 percent of avalanches occur on slopes between thirty and forty-five degrees. Steeper than that, and snow sloughs off before it can accumulate; shallower, and the tug of gravity is not so great. Avalanches occur most frequently right after big storms. Given time, snow tends to freeze together and stabilize.

Snow travels rapidly downhill in another way, too. Sudden melts occur when rain brought by tropical "Chinook winds" unleashes floods. Serious flooding in the Pacific Northwest is almost always a combination of rain and dissolving snow, occurring most frequently at the beginning and end of winter.

Scientists have been arguing for almost a century about how much logging and other land clearing contributes to snowpack scarcity and flooding problems. While studies dating back more than a century have suggested that heavy watershed logging can contribute to flooding, debate continues on whether trees conserve snowpack or intercept it.

The complication is that they do both. Snow will often linger in the shade of trees, melting slowly in early summer. On the other hand, the snow depth under trees is up to six times less than in open areas because branches intercept snow where it evaporates back into the sky. The darkness of forests also absorbs more solar radiation. Elk and deer often avoid clearings because the deep snow covers feed. They spend winter in deep forest where it's warmer and snow is shallower. So is tree cover a good thing or a bad thing if we want to preserve snowpack? Decades of research have established little more than that snowpack depth and duration hinge on many factors, and that human preference depends on when we want the water.

Certainly we expect water. In 1998, average per person consumption for Seattle Public Utility customers was one hundred and fifteen gallons per day, says Bruce Flory, senior economist for the department—enough to fill several bathtubs. The good news is that this thirst is down from one hundred and fifty gallons in 1989, a 23 percent decline. The bad news is that we use more than we can afford in drought years. As population grows, snow will likely become even more precious in years ahead.

Yet snow as resource, and snow as policy, really doesn't get to the root of our fascination with the stuff.

It's a midwinter psychological release. The first modern ski lift was built to accompany the first modern ski resort, at Sun Mountain, Idaho, in the 1930s, starting an industry so snow dependent that the first snow-making machines were introduced within twenty years of the ski lift. Ski slope snow in our Northwest is groomed like a lawn, tidied up after downhill skiers who can each shove a ton of snow out of place per day.

Nothing transforms the environment more quickly, or more magically, than snow. Its beauty is undeniable. Snowpack is necessary for the most arresting parts of our scenery, from Mount Rainier glaciers to wildflower meadows.

And what seems cold to us is a sheltering cocoon for over-wintering plants, crawling insects, and burrowing mammals. Snow itself is often rich in algae, bacteria, ice worms, fallen vegetation, dirt, bugs, and spiders.

A snowy mountain is a sculpture garden of depressions around the trunks of trees—fantastically flocked branches, sensuous drifts, and surface cups where pockets of dirt absorb sunlight and melt their own depressions.

A snow slope is an invitation to become a child again. The snowball fight is a childhood lesson on military escalation. A snowman, doomed to melt, is an edifice to the transience of life.

Andy Goldsworthy
Rivers & Tides

We respond viscerally to the beauty of snow, the quiet of snow, the light of snow, the threat of snow, the snugness of snow, the malevolence of snow, and the claustrophobia of snow. Our images range from the Christmas card to the destruction of Napoleon's and Hitler's armies in wintry Russia, from the sad peace of "Stopping by Woods on a Snowy Evening" to the haunted, snowbound lodge of _The Shining_.

If climate change does rob us of much of our snowpack, our Northwest will be a simpler and a poorer place, more vulnerable to drought and fire, less varied in its scenery, less watered and less lovely.

We can hope this won't occur. Knowing snow is at risk, we can take even more pleasure in the rare interruption of a Seattle snowstorm, the record-setting accumulations at Mount Baker and Mount Rainier, the splintery teeth of Mount Olympus's Blue Glacier, and the shocking cold of our stream pools still filling with meltwater in midsummer.

And there is something about snow that invites introspection, what a women's magazine in 1853 called "the moral teachings of snow." Novelist Peter Høeg equated the love of snow with falling in love and the knowledge of one's own death.

Poet Richard Hugo put it this way, in his "Snow Poem":

To write a snow poem you must ignore the snow
falling outside your window.

NORTHWEST ICONS

Cedar

THERE ARE CHURCHES IN THE PACIFIC
Northwest that have no walls, no pulpit, and no pews.
They are older than Notre Dame, as lofty as St. Peter's, and
as boundless as faith. Their choir is running water, their can-
dle a green, filtered sunlight, their prayer the creak and sigh
of branches rocking in rhythm to a winter wind. And their
location is secret, guarded by Native American tribes and
the U.S. Forest Service, which keeps a map so that sacred
sites are not mistakenly destroyed. So many are already gone,
you see. "Diminishing because of logging," laments Ernie
DeCoteau, cultural resources director of Washington's Sauk-
Suiattle tribe.

These churches are temples of cedar, the magic tree of
the Pacific Northwest. One of its Latin names is *arbor vitae*,
or "tree of life." No tree was, and is, more important to the
region's aboriginal inhabitants.

There is spirit power in dark groves of trees more than a
thousand years old. Natives still fast and bathe and seek visions
there. "You can receive that power," Lummi Indian spiritual-
ist Sam Cagey once assured, pointing to trees he said gave gifts
that sprang from the wood. "You can experience it yourself."

Ordinary cedar? Siding and fence wood? It seems improbable to modern eyes. The tree is not as tall as Douglas fir, not as numerous as hemlock, and not as strong as spruce. Hilary Stewart, in her book, *Cedar: Tree of Life to Northwest Indians*, calls its drooping look "weepy and woebegone . . . the lackadaisical giant with the softer heart."

But if not the biggest, then cedar was the most sacred and useful of all Northwest trees in aboriginal times, as central to the first inhabitants as salmon. Dismissed as structurally useless by early loggers, its increasing rarity has today turned it into red gold. Its price has doubled in recent years to more than a dollar a board foot at the mill, and more than that at the lumber store, if you can find it.

People sneak onto our national forests and risk fines and jail to cut shake blocks from old stumps because a cord that fills a pickup can bring eight hundred dollars. Steal an entire cedar that is tight-grained old growth and you've got a bootleg product worth almost enough to buy a luxury automobile. In Darrington, Washington, there's a Forest Service evidence locker with tagged blocks of recovered wood.

Cedar wasn't always so prized. Species fall in and out of favor in our society like Hollywood celebrities, depending on their glamour and utility at the moment. Whales, wolves, bears, and owls are famous examples. In aboriginal times, however, cedar was the central constant. The trees were hardware store, lumberyard, and clothing source. Cedar was used to make diapers, canoes, fishing nets, masks, houses, rope, and tools. Nothing else was so easily split, shed water so well, or resisted rot so reliably.

Its bark was stripped and pounded to make capes, hats, skirts, towels, baskets, sails, and cord for fishing nets. Its thin, wiry withes, or small branches, were braided to make cable.

Its trunk wood could be hollowed and stretched to make seaworthy canoes: one man sailed a thirty-eight-foot cedar canoe around the world at the turn of the century.

Cedar was bent to make boxes, shaped as beams and totem poles, split into planks for longhouses, or carved as masks, bowls, or spoons. Archeologists have found buried cedar artifacts older than Troy. Tribes were training cedar specialists when the carpenter Jesus walked the earth.

For craftsmen with stone tools, cedar had several advantages. Its soft wood was easier to chop than Douglas fir, meaning it was feasible for Native Americans to actually cut a cedar down. Even then it could still take three men up to three days to fell a tree. Sometimes they laboriously chiseled away like beavers, and sometimes they set fire to the easily burning base, protecting the upper tree from the flames with a barrier of wet clay. Alternately, cedar drift logs or trees that were carried downstream by rivers could be seized and used for construction.

Cedar was relatively light, making it easier to drag and lift. A series of wedges could split a log in place into usable planks, making transport even simpler. Cedar's cell structure allowed it to break along even planes. Its splinters could be polished smooth with sandstone or dogfish skin.

Because the tree grows in boggy places, cedar contains a natural, aromatic fungicide to resist rot and insects. Properly cared for, cedar siding can last as long as Seattle and Portland have been in existence. Cedar canoes were more easily hollowed, lighter to beach and paddle, and more resistant to decay than those of any other wood.

Bark clothing may strike us as odd, but it is no odder than the use of the cotton plant to make shirts or paper to make towels. Cedar cloaks were superior to furs in shedding rain. They dried quickly and could be oiled with bear grease and insulated with duck down. Captain Cook termed the cedar hats he found on Vancouver Island the best headgear he'd ever seen.

Women stripped cedar bark from young trees when the sap was running in spring and summer and turned it into products ranging from towels to tourniquets. Gnarled cedar roots were cut to make tools and fish hooks. Burls on the trunk became bowls. "Cedar was the K-Mart store for the Indians because it had everything in it," says Peter Selvig, forestry tech supervisor for the Darrington, Washington, ranger district. He uses the wood seized from cedar thieves to repair historic Forest Service buildings.

Some pioneers made homes by putting a roof on rotted-out cedar stumps. Modern society uses cedar primarily for siding, shakes, shingles, posts, decking, trim, and window frames. Old-growth cedar is a beautifully perfumed wood, the color of honey and amber, which without adornment suggests a rustic richness.

When Lindal Cedar Homes moved to Seattle from Canada in 1962, the wood was still so plentiful that the company's house walls were made of solid cedar, remembers chairman Robert Lindal. Today it's so dear in price that cedar is usually limited to siding and decorative trim, some of that from smaller second-growth trees artfully machined and joined to eliminate knots and make bigger pieces of lumber. Old-growth cedar is still being cut in British Columbia, but it's largely gone from Washington and Oregon. The Canadian province supplies two-thirds of the cedar sold in the United States.

Biologically, our cedar is not a true cedar at all. The famed Mediterranean tree that has biblical mention as the "cedars of Lebanon" doesn't grow here. And though our cedar's scientific name, *Thuja plicata,* means "false cypress folded in plaits," it's not really a cypress either. Our western red cedar is its own species, a unique and noble tree with the longevity to surpass Methuselah. One nearly two-thousand-year-old specimen at British Columbia's Cheewhat Lake was recorded at sixty-two feet in circumference and one-hundred-and-ninety-four-feet high. (That's tall — but the tallest Douglas fir on record was twice as high.)

Washington State is home to several cedars that vie for the national championship. Because the American Forest Association gives twelve times as many points to circumference as height, the current title-holder is the Quinault Lake Cedar on the north shore of Lake Quinault, measuring sixty-three and a half feet around and one hundred and fifty-nine feet high. Arguably bigger is the Nolan Creek cedar near Forks, sixty-one feet around and one hundred and seventy-eight feet high. A cedar on the Ohanepecosh River in Mount Rainier National Park is considerably taller at two hundred and thirty-four feet, but only twenty feet around. The Kalaloch cedar at Sixth Beach is the fattest, at sixty-four feet around, but only one hundred and twenty-three feet high. All have multiple tops because of the tendency for old cedar to break off and regrow.

Take your pick as your personal champion.

The smaller Alaskan, or yellow cedar, can be found at elevations above twenty-five hundred feet and has been prized as a boat-building wood. A near relative of that species, Port Orford cedar in southwestern Oregon, has long been considered one of the premier boat woods in the world.

While increasingly rare, cedar is a very resilient tree. Each conifer has a different strategy. Douglas fir sprouts best in full sunlight, and often dominates after forest fires or clearcuts. Hemlock grows in the shade of fir, eventually succeeding it. Cedar prefers dappled shade and wet places, and only rarely grows in groves of its own kind. Rather it's a mixer, opportunistically poking its way into the forest here and there, taking over from other conifers that don't want to get their feet wet. There is no cedar forest, but there are many cedar trees.

It's a beautiful tree but falls short of the nobility of fir or redwood or sequoia. Cedar's easily identified bark of papery strips looks a bit untidy, as if the tree needs some hair gel to lie down properly. Its needles are flat, its branches don't have the perky bristle of fir, and the whole tree seems to sag slightly, as if with the burden of age and wisdom. So well do the branches shed water that some Indians call it *shabalup*, or "dry underneath."

Nutrient and water passages in the wood leave cedar with a microscopic pattern of air spaces that make it light and a good insulator, similar to foam board.

And while some conifers shut down growth in the darkness of winter, cedar is more attuned to temperature than sunlight and will grow on a warm winter day.

While cedar prefers to have sex with other cedars, the tree is also capable of "selfing," a botanical term for self-pollination or, if you will, having sex with yourself. Scientists theorize this evolved as a survival strategy in the Ice Ages, allowing cedars cut off from their mates to continue to reproduce.

Most conifers avoid the in-breeding dilemma of selfing by having their female cones higher than their male, so that pollen won't reach. Alternately, they have two types of cones that mature at different times. At need, however, cedar will release a flood of yellow pollen from its male cones that can be received by females on the same tree, which in turn produce a prolific release of seed in the fall. Cedar cones are no bigger than a fingernail and their seeds are so tiny that they average about four hundred thousand to the pound. An acre of mixed trees can produce sixty million cedar seeds per year, only a few of which will ever germinate.

Humans don't typically associate plants with sex, but plants exchange genetic material just as animals do. So fecund are Northwest forests, with pollen and seed floating hither and yon, that it might stimulate one's interest in forestry to think of our mountainsides as one gigantic x-rated movie. Spring is suffused with pollen dust, and hillsides erupt with the red and yellow hues of plant sex.

Cedar grows slowly and long, one reason why it has not been replanted until recently. It's not uncommon for a cedar tree to reach a thousand years in age, and a few approach two thousand. When they fall, their rot-resistant logs can persist for centuries more. But cedar doesn't spurt in size, and it doesn't lend itself to monoculture tree plantations. Humans get impatient with it.

Cedar was once so abundant and worthless, Selvig recalled, that loggers would cut stronger firs to fall onto cedar and splinter it. The loggers thus avoided having to pay stumpage prices on the trees. Structurally weak, cedar was junk wood, good for shingles and kindling but too fast-burning even to make good firewood. Now the wood's price has prompted interest in its survival. Like alder, cedar is being replanted aggressively and harvested more carefully.

Native Americans never forgot cedar's value. They prize cedar for the bounty it offers and the secrets it contains. Each remaining grove is a sacred place as venerable as a gothic cathedral. We'll continue to use cedar industrially, as the Indians did, but we'll also increasingly use it spiritually. In it's utility, majesty, and longevity, cedar inspires a communion with nature as vital and relevant to modern society as it was to the aboriginal inhabitants.

Geoducks

SIZE MATTERS.

It matters to Asian seafood lovers, who pay retail prices up to thirty dollars a pound to dine on gargantuan neck of *Panopea abrupta*, better known by its Nisqually Indian name of *gwe-duk*, or "dig-deep": the geoduck.

That's "gooey-duck" to you newcomers.

Size matters, say we Northwesterners, who get bragging rights to the world's biggest burrowing clam. The geoduck can become an old-growth monster, living more than one hundred and fifty years and weighing up to twenty pounds.

Size matters, says Port Townsend, Washington, naturalist David George Gordon, author of *Field Guide to the Geoduck*, because the flesh and shell of geoducks combined make up one of the greatest biomasses of any animal in Puget Sound. "If you had a pile of all the salmon, and all the seals, and all the orca whales, and all the everything, the geoduck pile would be the biggest," he contends.

There are an estimated 130 million geoduck clams of adult size (about two pounds or bigger) in the state's harvest zone, in water between eighteen and seventy feet deep. That doesn't count the clams in shallower or deeper water: geoducks are found from the tide zone to depths of at least three hundred and fifty feet. There are probably 300 million to 400 million adult geoducks in Washington State alone, estimates Department of Natural Resources geoduck manager Ron Teissere, or more giant clams than there are people in the United States.

And size matters, because despite the geoduck's taste, abundance, and economic importance, it is the *appearance* of the geoduck that produces a certain kind of . . . awe. Curiosity. Wonder. Inadequacy.

Men gape. Women swoon.

Well, not swoon, exactly. They actually tend to gasp, snigger, gulp, snort, and smirk. Because a geoduck looks like — that is to say it sort of resembles — what we mean here is that it has evolved into a shape reminiscent of . . .

You know.

And therein lies our fondness for the beast. Funny name, funny shape, funny squirt. It's funny, like raw oysters.

What is it with mollusks, anyway?

Until relatively recently, much of what we knew about geoducks was summed up by "The Gooey Duck Song," a hymn to bivalves penned by Ron Konzak and Jerry Elfendahl:

Well, he hasn't got a front and he hasn't got a back,
He doesn't know Donald and he doesn't go 'quack,'
Digga duck, digga duck, digga digga gooey duck . . .

Washington's ever-liberal and irreverent Evergreen State College chose the geoduck as its mascot and adopted the motto *Omni extaris*, Latin for "Let it all hang out." They have a granite sculpture of a geoduck in their gym lobby which Athletic Director Pete Steilberg describes as "some-

what phallic," and an official "Fighting Geoducks" fight
song:

> *Go, geoduck, go, siphon high, siphon low . . .*

    In other words, most Northwesterners—having learned just
how hard it is to dig out a gigantic clam buried two to three
feet below the surface—are content simply to laugh at it.

    But not all, thanks to the Cold War. In the mid-1960s a
Navy diver from the Undersea Warfare laboratory at Keyport,
a man named Bob Sheats, was looking for a wayward test tor-
pedo near Bainbridge Island when he realized that Puget
Sound's muck below the low-tide line was a veritable forest
of jutting, gulping, spewing, and utterly unself-conscious

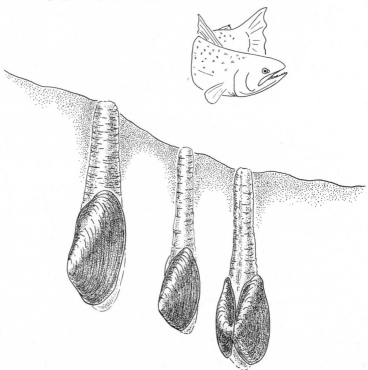

geoduck necks. The adult clams can congregate in densities as thick as one geoduck every two square feet.

Washington's state Fisheries Department (now Fish and Wildlife) confirmed the discovery, and the Department of Natural Resources claimed ownership on the grounds that geoducks were buried in its mud. Natural Resources is caretaker for Washington's underwater lands. Then the two agencies did what a state agency always does when it discovers a new resource: they wondered who they could sell it to.

The "who" initially were chowder companies, which paid as little as ten cents a pound. Then Washington King Clam, Inc., of Tacoma, which by 1980 accounted for 95 percent of the geoduck harvest, began marketing the clams in Asia. Here was this monster . . . *thing*, of incredible longevity, with a certain sexual . . . *charisma*. Mediocre in chowder, it was actually quite good as raw sushi. And it could be air-freighted to a continent newly flush with money. By the late 1980s, wholesale geoduck prices hit eight to ten dollars a pound, geoducks were being sold in Asian restaurants for three times that, and divers were using high-pressure air hoses to blast geoducks free of bottom mud like fifty-dollar bills.

Money made the geoduck respectable.

To keep the rest of us happy, half of the state's share of the geoduck money—it leases geoduck tracts to the highest bidder—goes into the Aquatic Lands Enhancement Account. This is used for projects ranging from wetlands preservation to new public docks and waterfront trails. Divers pay the state about three dollars a pound for the geoducks they harvest, earning about $6 million a year for Washington.

It's an American success story. But geoducks?

I would like to report that the geoduck is a noble and fascinating animal, brave, swift, and smart, a triumph of natural selection and evolutionary grace. Something other than just big, and vaguely obscene. Alas, geoduck drama peaks at conception and goes downhill, literally, from there. Spawning is admittedly impressive. Mollusks are called "bivalves" not because of their siphon-tube jets but because that's Latin for "two-door," referring to the hinged shell that encloses the animals. But their necks do have two main pipes, and a geoduck's plumbing is its *raison d'être*.

Geoducks eat and breathe by sticking this eyecatching appendage above the sand and sucking in water through one tube to extract its algae and oxygen. They spit water out the other. When algae seem particularly thick, geoducks seize the moment by releasing clouds of milky white sperm or grain-size eggs from their exhalant tube like a coordinated chorus of geysers. Fertilization hinges on current and fate.

"They're like little undersea volcanoes spewing genetic material into the water," says state fisheries biologist Bob Sizemore, a diver. Females release as many as ten batches of eggs a year, or fifty million potential geoducks apiece. The ladies are fecund for a century, meaning they can produce a whopping five billion eggs in their lifetime. Needless to say, you wouldn't want to write insurance policies on any one youngster's individual chances.

The fertilized egg becomes a floating larva propelled by waving tendrils, called *cilia*, which work like oars. For up to four weeks the larva drifts and swims around, eating algae and being eaten. Then, survivors having grown to the size of a grain of rice, the clam settles to the bottom with the beginning of its shell. It crawls with a developing foot, putting out threads to grip surrounding sand grains to help haul itself along. If it wants to float with the current, the threads are released to wave in the flow and carry the clam like a parachute.

This is by far the most active and perilous stage of a geoduck's life. It roams to find suitable places to begin burrowing deeper and deeper, seeking refuge from crabs, sea stars, dogfish, otters, and a host of other enemies. By the end of their second year the few surviving geoducks are big enough to dig down to "refuge depth" of two to three feet below the surface, where few predators can reach them.

And that's about it. The clam keeps growing until it's so big that its shell can't close around it, a not uncommon phenomenon of age, geoduck writers have noticed. The geoduck's foot becomes so small in relation to its body (it looks like a pitiful gray polyp) that it can no longer dig or move. For the next century or more, our hero becomes the ultimate couch potato.

By four years the adolescent clam is a harvestable two pounds. By fifteen years it has reached its maximum size. It's relatively safe, is insulated from temperature changes, and requires no energy to move or grow. It can subsist on remarkably little food and its body's few moving parts don't do much: geoducks simply don't wear out. No one really knows how long geoducks can live, but annual bands in the shell walls showed that one Vancouver Island specimen was one hundred and forty-six years old.

Personality? Well, geoducks have no brain, eyes, ears or, presumably, feelings. They are an organic machine, plumbing and pump. A few geoducks from the state shellfish lab at Brinnon on Hood Canal were given parts for the filming of the movie version of *Snow Falling on Cedars*, but they're the exception. Most lead lives of quiet anonymity.

Is that it, then? Is that all there is to the geoduck story? No. Geoduck fans should try Gordon's field guide, which provides considerably more biological detail than this essay.

The clam is a fascinating animal. In these pages we can add sex, money, violence, and greed to the saga.

Sex first. Once wholesale geoduck prices multiplied as much as one hundred times over two decades, the state and industry became interested in growing the clams artificially. Natural repopulation of a harvested bed can take thirty-five to fifty years, while artificial planting could cut the time needed for reharvest to five years.

But how do you hatch a geoduck? The secret is a dark room, good food, and soft music. "They're sensitive to light, sensitive to temperature, and sensitive to water," says Washington shellfish hatchery manager Amilee Caffey. To get the necessary squirt of eggs and sperm, adult geoducks are put in a tank in a dark room, fed a meal of the choicest algae, and serenaded (yes, romance still exists!) by Hawaiian love songs. The music was the idea of state fisheries biologist Hal Beattie, an impish sort who has pioneered methods of shellfish propagation. Then scientists wait, sometimes for hours. "If they don't spawn after a while, it's time to break out the wine and candlelight," Beattie quips. "By the time we finish the wine, we don't care anyway."

Caffey denies this story, which is a pity, and says scientists actually just try again the next day. Sooner or later they get enough fertilized eggs to start growing baby geoducks. The state's biggest tanks can hold forty million geoduck larvae. The original, not illogical, plan was to grow a bunch of baby clams and pitch them over the side of a boat. Unfortunately, crabs gobbled seeded geoducks faster than the state hatched them. "We weren't planting, we were feeding," laments Beattie. The state yanked the money from that experiment. Today, the empty concrete tanks of Brinnon are sad monuments to science unrequited.

Biologists persisted, however. In Washington, geoducks are now hand planted on tide flats inside short lengths of protective PVC pipe and are covered with mesh to keep out predators. Once the clams are big enough to dig to refuge depth, the pipe is removed and used again. In British Columbia, experiments are underway with a machine that plants geoducks below the low-tide mark and covers them with mesh.

Taylor Shellfish Farms of Shelton, Washington, plants 3.5 million geoducks a year. Its first pioneering five-year-olds brought top dollar because young geoducks tend to have whiter necks, highly prized in Asia.

Which brings us to money, greed, and violence. A prime geoduck of moderate weight has brought as much as a hundred dollars in Hong Kong or Tokyo, which means the temptation to monopolize, poach, and cheat can be irresistible. King Clam was accused of trying to monopolize the market with phony bidders in the early 1980s. Then, widespread poaching in a poorly regulated industry led to a federal investigation called "clam scam" in 1982.

A 1992 court decision recognizing Indian treaty rights to half the shellfish harvest led to other claims of initial abuse when tribal members first joined the clam rush. And in 1997, a Las Vegas shellfish broker pleaded guilty to putting out a five thousand dollar contract to have a rival beaten up by a three hundred pound geoduck diver, an assault that never took place but is awesome to imagine. A year later, six divers and seafood brokers were arrested in a new black-market investigation.

In response to all this, Washington State and the tribes have sharply increased harvest supervisory staff. The market has stabilized, and Indians now dive for 1.5 million pounds of geoducks annually, earning $7.5 million in gross revenue. The policing hasn't halted criticism of the geoduck fishery. Property owners complain the air compressors on boats are noisy, and that what Washington has invented amounts to underwater clearcutting. Mining of underwater clams can strip a bed, destroy other mud-dwelling marine life, fill the water with disturbed sediment, and leave behind a wasteland that might not recover for half a century.

Some divers and critics warn that Washington is making the same mistakes with geoducks it made with timber and salmon: overharvest of the oldest and best clams, their replacement with younger ones, poor replanting, hatchery production that risks genetic weaknesses, and so on. "They manage it strictly for economics, not for the resource," complains diver John Lentz, who has been harvesting geoducks since 1983.

In response, Washington officials have commissioned mathematically impressive analyses of geoduck reproduction, and University of Washington scientists are studying clam genetics to avoid mistakes. Still, divers have lobbied for legislation to limit harvest licenses and force more state replanting. State officials respond that divers are seeking to keep competitors out and force their own hire for planting.

About the only side that isn't yelling is the geoducks'. "People are grouchy over salmon," explains Gordon. "They have this paranoia that we'll have the same problems with geoducks."

Lentz makes one point with which none would disagree. Geoduck harvesting is hard, cold, dangerous work. Divers work with an air hose to the surface that can periodically kink, they struggle with high-pressure hoses to break the clams loose, and they work in a murky twilight.

Yet a good diver can average five hundred to one thousand pounds a day, and Lentz has had days of four-thousand-pound catches. Even at the diver catch rate of thirty-five or forty cents a pound, that's good money.

The growing harvest certainly suggests that the geoduck has yet to receive its full due in our Northwest. Here is the mightiest saltwater animal (in biomass, at least) of our marine ecosystem, but where are its bronze statues, thrusting toward the sky? Why, when geoducks crowd the markets of Asia, do prodigious specimens not face shoppers in the aisles of Safeway? Where are the cooking shows, the tasting tables, the geoduck derbies? You can find geoducks at Seattle's Asian food stores, yes, but they've become rare even in the city's Pike Place Market. For shame!

May I modestly suggest gubernatorial recognition, expensive public relation campaigns, geoduck queens, and a geoduck look-alike contest? Let the world's biggest burrowing clam become the proud symbol of our Northwest id.

But dig one? Nah. Too gwe-duk.

Crabs

IF THE CRAB DID NOT EXIST, THE COMIC book would have to invent it.

The crab is horrifyingly beautiful in a space-alien kind of way, clever and amusing in its sideways scuttle, armored like a robot, defended by claws that bring to mind Popeye's forearms, and all-seeing with its complex eyes extended on stalks. What animal is better as a Pacific Northwest superhero?

Certainly, any crab is a survivor against fantastic odds. It may be the lone survivor of a brood of two million brothers and sisters released into the water by its mother. This clan is thinned by a hundred enemies through its many stages of life, and survival is rare. Supercrab has beaten the odds just by being here.

A crab can also boast that it's a true blueblood. Its color is dictated by the copper that it carries in its veins instead of iron.

If a crab loses an appendage like an arm or antenna, it will eventually regrow it. Spiderman can't do that.

And to grow in general, the animal has to conduct an escape act that would baffle Houdini. Confined by its existing shell, it must grow a new one to get bigger. It pries open the rear of its old shell and backs out, legs, claws and all, meaning that the soft tissue of its enormous front claw has to be pulled out through the tight casement of the skinny leg, a feat of dexterity worthy of a rubber pretzel.

The temporarily soft-shelled crab then buries itself in mud for protection, swells with seawater to become about 15 percent larger than its former size, and begins growing its new armor. Eventually its muscles and organs will completely fill its roomier house and it will have to molt all over again—about once a year for a full-grown Dungeness crab, which can live seven or eight years.

Our Northwest crab superhero would have to be a Dungeness, of course, a commercial species found from Alaska to California but especially plentiful off Washington and Oregon. Any true wet-sider knows at least three things: rain is good for you; you don't put a "the" in front of Puget Sound; and Northwest Dungeness crabs are the best in the world. The distinctive meat leaves no room for argument. You either love it or you need professional help. The messy effort required to get at the flesh only adds to its desirability.

It deters enthusiasts only a little that our hero, the crab, is essentially a big bug. Crabs are a ten-legged relative of insects, and both kinds of bugs are part of a group of animals called arthropods. Instead of a skeleton and spine, the arthropods have an exterior shell, or carapace, that encloses all their mushy stuff. Ugly? Admittedly so. Awkward? They are if they have to molt. But the cuts and bruises we human have to worry about, because we resemble walking water balloons, are unlikely for this group of creatures. Their biological design is the most successful in the world, with well more than a million species using the armored architecture of arthropods.

Crabs, shrimp, and lobsters belong to a subgroup of arthro-

pods called the decapod crustaceans, which means, "ten-legged crusty marine things." A crab is essentially a shortened shrimp, with its tail (yes, crabs have tails) tucked under it. They are found almost everywhere in the world's oceans, from the deep sea to the high-tide mark.

There are far more crabs in the Northwest than people. Just how many more is unclear and depends in part on whether you're counting the trillions of larvae hatched each winter, or the mere millions of adults that survive by fall. Besides Dungeness crabs—*Cancer magister* is the scientific name—Puget Sound and the coastal bays of Washington and Oregon host such species as red rock crabs, kelp crabs, hermit crabs, shore crabs of assorted colors, spider crabs (one species near Japan can reach ten feet from leg tip to leg tip), porcelain crabs (so named because their claws break off easily), horse crabs, and the Puget Sound king crab, which can weigh up to ten pounds and differs from the commercial Alaskan variety.

Scientists such as Paul Dinnel, a consultant to Western Washington University's Shannon Point Marine Center in Anacortes, Washington, have counted ten to twenty young adult crabs per square meter in some bays. The count is less encouraging in the industrial harbors of the Northwest, where dredging routinely destroys crab habitat. At Grays Harbor on Washington's coast, researchers have tried depositing oyster shells on the bottom to provide new shelter after dredging. The effort has been only partly successful.

Still, enough crabs survive in Washington alone to sustain a commercial and recreational catch of up to a million crabs each year in the state's inland waters, and from two to twenty million crabs off the Northwest coast. Generally, the recreational catch is only about one percent of the commercial harvest. Despite the big harvest, our superhero's numbers rise and fall primarily in response to natural cycles only barely understood. When conditions are right, Northwest waters can grow a lot of crab. When they aren't, the catch plummets.

The commercial appeal of crab is obvious. They bring good money. Their biological appeal is a bit subtler, since they admittedly look like monsters. It takes a person such as Greg Jensen, a marine biologist at the University of Washington and author of *Pacific Coast Crabs and Shrimps,* to explain why anyone (other than another crab) could fall in love with the beasts.

Actually, crab love is a good place to start in discussing their appeal. Porcelain crabs, for example, are sweetly monogamous, pairing off and refusing to mate with anyone else. Unless, scientists have found, a mate is removed for more than three days, by which time its partner will have forgotten its paramour. Dungeness crab love is less romantic. Females release smell particles in the water during the spring and a mating stampede is on. A congregation of females can put the males in such frenzy that their ardor fixes on whatever is available. Jensen observed one poor fellow trying to mate with an empty Dr. Pepper can.

Crabs are admirably shifty. They have tiny hairs on their shells that detect water movement as an early-warning system. "The crab hasn't seen you, but it has felt you approaching," Jensen says. Most crab species run sideways because of the arrangement of their legs. Scientists suspect crabs evolved that way because such sidling tended to confuse predators.

Crabs also have two brains, one at the front end and another at the rear to help control its legs. "I think crabs are smarter than we give them credit for," says Jensen. He's watched them improve their technique of cracking a mollusk shell when a new species of shellfish is introduced into a tank, and then remember the method. In other words, they can learn. Crabs also seem able to use their insectlike antennae to recognize other crabs.

If our superhero loses a limb, the broken spot is swiftly closed to prevent bleeding and a replacement begins to grow with each molt. If you find a crab with a leg or claw smaller than the others, it's probably a replacement appendage growing in stages back to normal size. And if you find a crab shell, it's not evidence of our hero's mortality. Because crabs molt, the "dead" crab found by excited children may actually be only a discarded suit of armor. If the shell has decaying, smelly flesh inside it, it's a dead crab, but if the shell is light and relatively odorless, the crab lives on. Biologists call such discards "pop-tops" because the rear of the shell pops open where the growing crab crawls out.

The life cycle of a crab is a fascinating story of transformation. Larval crab look so different from adults that scientists initially thought they were an entirely different animal. For Dungeness, it all starts when females mate after molting. A hard-shelled male attracted by the scent she releases will grapple her from behind and remain attached for up to a week before mating takes place. He isn't a leech. The soft-shelled future mother is vulnerable to predators at this time, and the male helps ward off rivals and enemies. After mating the female will bury herself in sand for protection until her new shell hardens, with just her eye stalks protruding above the bottom. The male will stand watch for up to two days. If danger approaches he will move to meet it, but he will always keep at least one leg in contact with the female to maintain his claim. His sperm is stored for later fertilization of her eggs, which usually occurs from October through December. Because of this lengthy lag time, the issue of paternity could become confused. Accordingly, some species of crabs plug the genitals of the female with a hard substance to keep any other male from mating with her.

The female subsequently produces one to two million eggs, each the size of a grain of salt, fertilizing them from a sperm-storage chamber and depositing them on the flapping tail of her abdomen. She takes care to ensure that adequate water circulates to aerate the eggs while they grow. As the eggs hatch in winter, she rises up on the tips of her legs and thrusts her abdomen to release larvae into the water. For a few minutes the larvae retain their egg casing so they will bounce away from the hard, jagged surface of the mother without harm. Then they rapidly develop spines to make them less palatable to the fish that feed on them. The spiny larvae can drift in clouds so dense that they've lodged in the gills of farmed salmon and have contributed to net-pen fish kills.

Tidal current pulls the larvae out to sea. If they drift too far, the crabs won't be able to get back to shallow water to develop as juveniles, and crabbing will be poor several years down the road. If they find lots of plankton to eat and encounter fewer predators, future crabbing will be good.

Larvae begin developing the buds that will become legs and claws. By spring the schools of surviving young have developed to a shrimplike stage called megalops, but they are still no bigger than large mosquitoes. Ideally, they drift back toward shore and congregate in shallow bays where the scent from adults indicates a suitable habitat. Generally a bed of sand, gravel, and seaweed or eelgrass is ideal as a crab nursery. Even if they survive to this point, a crab's chance of living to full adulthood is about as likely as buying a winning lottery ticket. Larvae, megalops, and young crab are prey for fish, gulls, starfish, and octopus. If they survive to the ripe old age of two or three, however, crabs have reached a respectable size and are so encased by shell that they've become the armored truck of the seabed. By age four, they are reaching the 6.25-inch minimum legal size for harvesting and are scavenging dead meat and dining more frequently on shellfish.

Cracking mollusks for a meal is the primary purpose of those big claws, though they are also used for display and fighting. Crabs have six more appendages near their mouth to help them eat with an intricacy that is both delicate and creepy. Various crab species have different preferred foods and different strategies. Some move up a beach at high tide to dig for shallowly buried shellfish, working quickly before retreating into the water. Others stay at greater depth but have to work harder to get at mollusks buried deeper, because there's no receding tide to keep predators away. A commonly observed species is shore crabs, which can be exposed at low tide by flipping over rocks on a cobble beach. They feed on plant or animal detritus and stay under rocks to be protected from heat, freshwater rain, and predators like birds. Red rock crab and Puget Sound king crab, in contrast, prefer the rocky underwater cliffs of the San Juans.

A good deal of what goes on in the sea remains a mystery. So unexplored is the underwater world that Jensen has been able to discover and describe several new species of shrimp in his dives in Puget Sound and the San Juans. What *is* known is that crabs are as important as they are successful. They are food for a host of creatures, and in turn they feed themselves on just as many. We are right to protect them, not just because of nostalgic affection for our comic heroes or appreciation of their weird, multicolored beauty, but because they're vital in maintaining the healthy ecology of the deep.

Despite this, crabs have an image problem. To be described as "crabby" is to be criticized, crab apples are sour, to "catch a crab" when rowing is to mishandle the oar, and the Latin word for crabs, *cancer*, which is also one of the constellations of the Zodiac, has gone from its root meaning of "hardness" to association with the tough tumors of a dreaded disease. "Crabs" is the appelation of lice we're embarrassed to harbor, and "crabbed" writing describes the penmanship of misers and lunatics.

Yet, as with the geoduck, it's not too late for a makeover here in our Northwest. Roland Anderson, Puget Sound biologist, calls the Puget Sound king crab "a gentle giant, slow living and slow growing." That sounds like a pretty good image improvement for the group as a whole. It all depends on how you look at them. So watch the intricate scurry of their ten legs at the aquarium, study their bizarre countenance at the fish counter, and contemplate the astounding variety of nature when cracking into one at a waterfront restaurant. You might even conclude that they're beautiful. For a bug.

Cougars

THE COUGAR SAW BRUCE RICHARDS WITH its great yellow eyes before he saw her. She smelled him first and heard him first. A clumsy two-leg, blundering toward her cubs in thick December brush in the Green River watershed east of Puget Sound. The game agent was looking for a radio collar he thought might be on a dead animal. The cougar hadn't moved for days. Now the signal was moving again, confusing the human as she stalked him in a low crawl, her ears back, her chin on the ground, her muscles bunched. "It hadn't dawned on me that she might have made a den to have cubs," he recalls. It hadn't occurred to him that he was venturing toward the lair of a defensive mother.

Here was an evolutionary mismatch: Richards stumbling toward the most successful and widespread carnivore in the Western Hemisphere, the perfect killing machine of the Pacific Northwest, an animal to make the heart hammer. A cougar can sprint twice as fast as an Olympic athlete, jump higher than a second-storey balcony, tackle an elk five times its weight, and bite with one ton of force per square inch. Its teeth are spaced perfectly to sever the neck vertebrae of deer.

All Richards had was a determination not to kill the magnificent animal—and his pistol.

The mother cat didn't know enough to be frightened of guns. Her initial charge stopped short at the noise, but she looked at a warning bullet that bounced off a boulder with more curiosity than fear. Richards jumped up on a stump to reload. He yelled, screamed, and howled like a dog. She hissed and snarled in reply.

"Finally I took off running," he recalls. "I turned around and she was coming after me in twenty and thirty foot leaps." He tripped in a creek, fired again, and then suddenly she was gone as swiftly as she came, retreating to her young. The game agent was drenched with sweat and quivering from adrenaline. His muscles ached from the tension.

"I saw him the next day and he looked like someone had hit him all over with a rubber mallet," said Rocky Spencer, another Washington state wildlife biologist.

Richards had seen the power of the wild that few of us ever experience. Yet the game agent had the guts to go back into the brush to retrieve a radio receiver he'd dropped, knowing the mother cougar would move on with her cubs to safety. "The chance of a tree limb falling on you in the woods is still much greater than being attacked by a mountain lion," he explains.

And statistically the evolutionary mismatch is in *our* favor. The last Washingtonian to be killed by a cougar was an Okanogan boy in 1924. In the entire nation, there have been only twelve recorded fatalities in the last one hundred and eight years. By comparison, scientists estimate up to a quarter-million cougars have been slain by humans since the arrival of Europeans.

To spot one remains a rare gift. Yet not so rare as it used

to be. Cougar numbers are rising. State officials estimate that the twenty-four hundred counted in Washington State in the year 2000 are increasing by at least fifty additional cats per year. At the same time, the human population is increasing by one hundred thousand per year. In short, we've launched a fascinating ecological experiment: the uneasy coexistence of Washington's two top predators, humans and the cougar. Can we tolerate an animal swifter, stealthier, and fiercer than ourselves as a neighbor? Can we embrace risk in the wild?

The issue was crystallized not long ago when a Colorado woman in a new subdivision called to complain of a bear in her backyard. "That's funny," the game warden replied. "I just got a call from a bear complaining there's a house in his *front* yard."

Cougar is a word that comes from the Brazilian Indians, making obvious the range of an animal that roams from the northern Canadian forests to the tip of South America. The same species is also called the mountain lion (from Europeans who thought it looked like a smaller version of the female African lion), puma (an Inca word), panther (of Latin and

Greek origin, applied to dark-colored leopards), painter (a Southern twist on panther), and catamount (New Englandese for "cat on a mountain").

For centuries the cats were feared and hated. Theodore Roosevelt called them "craven and cruel," an attribution of human emotions to an animal that has none. Washington State put a bounty of thirty-five dollars on the cats in the Great Depression, and as many as three hundred were killed per year. By the time the bounty ended in 1960, Washington cougars were rare. Oregon has a similar history.

Since then, the population has been rebounding by about 2 percent a year. As houses march into the foothills, complaints about problem cougars are rising, more than doubling since the mid-1990s. Livestock dead, pets devoured, cougars in backyards, cougars on porches, cougars near schoolyards.

In 2000, Washington's legislature overturned an initiative that had been passed by nearly two-thirds of voters just four years before: they now voted to reinstate hound hunting of problem cougars. The vote was in response to disturbing news. A cougar had preyed on captive wildlife at Northwest Trek, near Eatonville, Washington, before being trapped and relocated. A cougar in a Seattle suburb had killed a family dog and severely injured three state-owned hunting dogs before being shot. Cougars were spotted in the cities of Bellevue, Olympia, and Everett. A cougar was killed a block from a Leavenworth, Washington, elementary school. Of seven recorded nonfatal attacks on humans in Washington this century, six occurred in the 1990s. The mauling of a boy in the northeast corner of the state in 1998 tipped political opinion against the cats.

One reason for the cougar resurgence is an increase in deer and elk. While many hunters have long assumed that predators control the number of prey, and that cougars are competitors of human hunters, biological studies suggest the opposite. Cougar numbers rise and fall in relation to the number of deer. "Cougars assist in maintaining a balance," explains Steve Pozzanghera, a state wildlife manager.

There are two views of this cat comeback. Among urbanites, cougars have gone from horror-story villain to wilderness nobility, the same rehabilitation of reputation enjoyed by the wolf, the killer whale, and the grizzly bear. They epitomize the wild. When 63 percent of Washington voters elected to end hound hunting of cougars in 1996, they had decided the practice of treeing cougars with radio-collared dogs and then shooting them out of the tree was slaughter, not sport.

Some hunters counter that the cougar population is getting dangerously out of control. "I think we're going to have a tragedy if we wait too long," says B. J. Thorniley of Nordland, a president of Washingtonians for Wildlife Conservation, a hunting group. Cougars have recently killed people in California, Colorado, and Vancouver Island. To hunt a population that is thriving, Thorniley argues, is not cruel but "pays homage." Hounds afford the only practical, safe hunting method. Thorniley saves the pelt and eats the meat. Cougar, she reports, tastes good.

Game agents didn't like the outright ban on the use of hounds either. "I'm not comfortable with wildlife management at the ballot box," said Spencer. Yet the ultimate effect of hunting or hunting bans is unclear because of the complex habits of these cats. It's possible that slaying cougars makes coexistence worse, not better.

A cougar is not a huge animal. Females average about a hundred pounds and males about one hundred and forty-five, though one record-holder grew to two hundred and seventy-five pounds. They stand about two feet high at the shoulder and their bodies are up to five feet long, tails stretching that to eight feet. They have excellent night vision and they use twice as many brain cells as we do for smell. They use whiskers that are the same width as their body to gauge which holes they can squeeze into.

Female cougars generally mind their own business because, in cougar culture, the mother looks after the cubs. The female can come into heat at any time of the year and will mate several hundred times over a period of up to eight days with a seemingly inexhaustible male, both giving a deeper, louder, and more disturbing version of the yowl of mating house cats. Three months later she gives birth to from one to six cubs, or kittens.

The newborns are irresistibly cute: born blind, they weigh a pound and have spots on their fur. Mother first nurses her litter, then weans it to meat, then teaches it how to hunt. One of the first cub targets is the dark spot at the end of her twitching tail. Biologists have also watched mothers teaching cubs to pounce on grasshoppers. They advance to bigger and bigger prey. When the juveniles are two years old, she drives them away toward new territory.

At first glance a male's life looks easier: no cubs to care for and the opportunity to mate in turn with six or seven females who share a single male's territory of more than a hundred thousand acres. Males, however, are in a constant war with one another to dominate this kingdom and its harem. Combat is savage, and most males don't survive the first few years of life. Spencer once found a male cougar skull bitten through by the powerful jaw of a rival.

Most juvenile males lose to older, bigger rivals and are frequently pushed into our suburban fringe. Still unskilled in stalking deer, these frustrated "teenagers" can be reduced by hunger into hunting livestock, pets, or even vulnerable-looking humans. Biologists have speculated that joggers killed in California might, when they bent to tie a shoe, have looked momentarily like deer.

We might assume that if fewer cougars are hunted, there will be more cats and more clashes with humans. But reality is not that simple. A study in Idaho, comparing wilderness populations of cougars with those closer to people, suggests that hunting may create as many problems as it solves. The wilderness group had smaller litters, which resulted in less battling among males, and more stability in the group. When humans killed cats, females gave birth to more cubs, resulting in a faster turnover of dominant males and a more restless population of male juveniles preying on domestic pets. In short, it's possible that a permanent ban on cougar hunting could ultimately create better coexistence.

We do know that cougars long predate any human habitation of the Western Hemisphere. They prefer to be left alone, often hunting in the dark and sleeping by day. They adapt to climates ranging from arctic to tropical, and to elevations from sea level to fifteen thousand feet in the Andes. Like big cats worldwide, their habits of hunting, sleeping, and mating are similar to those of house cats.

The binocular vision of their forward-set eyes lets cougars judge distance to calibrate their pounce. They strike quickly, because their relatively small lungs mean that they must catch their prey in a quick burst or lose the chase. Cougars kill every seven to ten days, eating about ten pounds of meat per day when fully grown. That implies an average take of about thirty deer a year, but biologists have observed cats varying from ten to ninety deer annually, depending on availability, climate (because meat spoils faster in heat), and competition. Sometimes cougars are chased from kills by wolves or bear and have to hunt again.

The mountain lions dine first on organs such as the liver that deliver vitamins they otherwise lack. They don't chew their food, relying instead on their powerful digestive system to break down chunks of meet. Their tongue has the same rough texture as a house cat's, useful for both grooming and to strip bones of meat. Typically a kill is only partly eaten and is then dragged and buried for later feasting. No cougar kill is "wasted," however. What the cats don't eat feeds an ecosystem of birds, ground scavengers, and decomposers.

Cougars serve to regulate deer populations, preventing overpopulation that can lead to famine and collapse. The cats' own numbers level off in balance with their prey. Biologists estimate Washington's cougar population, if unchecked, would peak at four thousand animals at most.

Given their huge territories, cougars probably find one another by smell. The most likely sign of a cougar that a hiker might encounter is a small mound of dirt and tree needles scraped together on a trail and scented by urine or scat. It both marks territory and alerts potential mates. The chance of hikers seeing a wild cougar is remote, however, and the glimpse is likely to be fleeting. "Mostly what you see are just these two big eyes, staring at you," says Spencer.

The standard advice if stalked is *never run*: this only signals that you are prey. If you are threatened, stand tall, shout, throw rocks or get a stick. Back away slowly, and fight if attacked. Cougars are reluctant to risk injury and will usually break off a hard fight for easier game.

More likely you'll see nothing, making do with the satisfaction that these predators are still thriving in our modern world. Cougars are neither good nor bad, they simply are. Your chance of being killed by one is smaller than your being killed by falling out of bed or being struck by lightning. They merely reinforce our sense of the wild as a place in which we are guests, instead of lords.

Cougars, after all, usually allow us clumsy two-legs to pass unmolested. "The majority of people have never seen a mountain lion," says Spencer. "But the lions have seen them. They're curious, like a cat, and they watch us."

And that, in the Pacific Northwest, still stirs the heart.

Bald Eagles

E ACH WEDNESDAY IN THE WETTEST DEPTHS
of the Northwest winter, tax attorney Tim Johnson for-
goes his practice in a rural suburb of Seattle, forgets the intri-
cacies of Internal Revenue codes, shuts up his house, climbs
into his pickup, and drives along the Stillaguamish River
between Darrington and Arlington to tally a count of the bald
eagle.

A typical stop is a scramble across river sloughs, the water
shuddering from the death throes of gray, spawned-out chum
salmon. The "Stilly" is the color of steel, and Whitehorse
Mountain rears its snow-powdered face into swirling clouds.
Stabs of winter sunlight are setting fire to the last lingering
leaves, and the eagles are back, their numbers peaking in early
January.

Johnson is one of a cadre of Nature Conservancy and
North Cascade Institute volunteers who use car, canoe, and
rubber boots to help check on the eagle population of northwest Washington. Libby Mills of Bayview has been doing so
for almost two decades, taking her love of the bird into class-
room presentations that enthrall children about this cycle in
regional ecology.

What draws these enthusiasts is an annual show of feathered magnificence that is aloof, brooding, amusing, striking, and finally reassuring. Canadian and Alaskan bald eagles fly south each year to dine on the spawned-out salmon of the Nooksack, Skagit, Sauk, and Stillaguamish rivers. Their return, Mills notes, "is a sign that the environment is in good health."

If fact, eagle numbers are growing. Are we humans finally doing something right? Groups such as The Nature Conservancy and Skagit Land Trust have joined with the state departments of Natural Resources and Fish and Wildlife, the U.S. Forest Service, and Seattle City Light to set aside nearly eight thousand acres of winter habitat along the Skagit River alone. Elsewhere around western Washington and Oregon, in gestures grand and small, timber companies, farmers, land developers, and hunters have made additional donations and concessions to help save a bird unique to North America.

And it's working. Bald eagle numbers in the contiguous forty-eight states reached their nadir in 1963, when only four hundred and seventeen nesting pairs were counted. Since then the population has rebounded to about fifty-three hundred pairs, and the eagle was removed from the endangered species list in 1998.

This success story starts with volunteers like Johnson and Mills. Or, more specifically, it started with a single volunteer named Charles Broley, a retired Canadian banker living in Florida who, in 1939, began to count the eagle nests along the Gulf Coast as a late-life hobby. By 1946, this Audubon Society bird watcher had found one hundred and forty nests that produced one hundred and fifty new eaglets that spring. Our national symbol was alive and well, it seemed.

Then the bottom fell out.

The pesticide DDT was one of the wonder chemicals to

emerge from World War II, and it began to be sprayed in vast, fogging clouds. As a result, eagle numbers collapsed. By 1952, there were only eleven active nests left in Broley's survey area. In 1962, biologist Rachel Carson published *Silent Spring*, a book warning that pesticides were annihilating the nation's bird population. Carson died of cancer before her warning could be verified. But scientists subsequently learned that the insecticide was washing into water and accumulating in fish that eagles ate. This inhibited calcium production in females, resulting in eggshells so weak that the parents inadvertently crushed their young before they could hatch. Some eagles simply went sterile.

from 140
in 1946

In 1972, DDT was banned in the United States. That decision was the most important in a series of steps to bring the eagle back. Congress had halted most hunting of bald eagles in 1940. In the 1980s, one hundred and twenty-four bald eagles were artificially incubated and released from Maryland. And in 1991, the U.S. Fish and Wildlife Service completed the phase-out of lead shot in hunter's ammunition, eliminating another source of wildlife poisoning.

Now the birds are back, although so much DDT was

released into the environment that residual concentrations in the mud of the lower Columbia River continue to depress wildlife numbers there. If eagle monitors such as Charles Broley—and Tim Johnson and Libby Mills—hadn't kept track, the peril might not have been noticed at all until it was too late.

Why all the fuss?

The bald eagle is today a glamourous bird and a color-crayon delight: snow white on its head and tail, black on its body, and bright yellow on its beak, eyes, and talons. Beauty counts in this world. Nonetheless, the bald eagle had long been a controversial bird, despised as a scavenger and bully. Benjamin Franklin bemoaned its choice as our national symbol in 1782, asserting: "He is a bird of bad moral character; he does not get his living honestly." The eagle was little more than a pretty buzzard, Franklin complained, eating the dead or stealing the catch of others. The patriot preferred the turkey.

John James Audubon so disliked eagles for their habit of harassing other birds that he wrote, "I grieve that it should have been selected as the emblem of my country."

Such criticism was not really fair, but it stuck. Because eagles were observed eating the flesh of dead livestock it was falsely assumed they were capable of killing farm animals. Although a full-grown eagle is capable of lifting no more than four pounds, there were myths that eagles could snatch babies, or at least lambs. The birds seemed a threat.

And for all their dignity, eagles have a habit of undignified hopping about the riverbank with driblets of decaying flesh hanging from their three-inch beaks, which is not something you want your national symbol to do. Style counts, too.

Accordingly, Americans didn't just poison their national bird; they were paid bounties to shoot it. Some one hundred

(100) and twenty-eight thousand were shot in Alaska alone from
1917 to 1952, where they were derided as "white-headed
crows" that preyed on marketable salmon. (Alaska still has
forty thousand bald eagles.) Thousands upon thousands
more were shot and poached from Washington to Texas.
Scientists estimate there may have been as many as half a million bald eagles in the Lower 48 when Europeans arrived.
Now we celebrate that we're back to one percent of that.

Despite this near extermination, eagles have been
acclaimed as much as they've been reviled. They have a fierce-
ness of eye that a professional wrestler would envy, talons that
can crush small bones, and a wingspan of six to eight feet.
Native Americans have revered bald eagles. The eagle's Old
World cousins were adopted as a symbol by the Egyptians,
Romans, Russians, Turks, Austrians, and Poles.

Not to mention Nazi Germany, the Depression's National
Recovery Administration, or the masthead of the *Seattle
Times*. Publisher Frank Blethen, who insisted on the eagle's
return to the paper, boasts an eagle tattoo on his leg.

Sea eagles—the generic name for these birds that nest,
roost, and forage near water—arose in Asia about twenty million years ago. There are sixty species in the world today. None
is more striking than the American bald eagle. "They are
incredibly cool birds," sums up Steve Negri, endangered
species biologist of the Washington Department of Fish and
Wildlife. And cool is the operative word. They have presence,
star quality, panache.

The bald eagle has lived in North America for a million
years. Its early colonial name comes from archaic English,
in which the Latin-rooted *blanc*, or white, became corrupted
to *balde*, meaning not a hairless head but an older, wiser, white
one. Their distinctive coloring is a mark of sexual maturity

and allows bald eagles to recognize each other at recorded distances of up to forty miles. Their vision is four times as powerful as ours, so only viewing an eagle through binoculars gives an idea of the acuity with which they can see you.

Their night vision is poor, however, which is the reason that during winter they roost, or sleep overnight, in selected stands of trees on northeast slopes or in swampy bottomlands away from the worst of the wind. Negri works hard to identify roost sites because they can be easily lost to logging. Washington's wintering eagle population can total more than a thousand birds but could decline sharply if roosting sites are lost. This migrant population leaves in spring for nesting areas as far away as the Yukon and Alaska's Copper River.

Besides these migrants there is a separate population of resident bald eagles in the state, with about six hundred counted nests. Figuring a pair of birds per nest, that means there is a resident state population of about twelve hundred adult birds, plus a fluctuating number of juveniles. While more than half of these nest in five counties in northwestern Washington, eagles are found in more and more locales and are proving surprisingly adaptable. Nests have been built throughout metropolitan Seattle. Some of these resident eagles stay the winter while others fly farther south, even as cousins from Canada and Alaska take their place. Why the birds migrate so far, when suitable feed could be found much closer to their nest areas, remains a biological mystery.

The nice thing about eagles is that we notice them. They are big, and when their mottled juvenile plumage gives way to adult coloration, they are one of the easiest birds to recognize. They soar with a stately glide, giving us time to take them in, and they indulge in amazing acrobatics. Eagles can briefly fly upside down to snatch a fish from the talons of an

202 / NORTHWEST ICONS

osprey, and they have dive-bombed snoozing sea otters to grab food from their paws. They indulge in a spectacular courtship ritual in which male and female will lock talons and spiral downward with an audible whir of wind, releasing and gliding away just moments before striking the ground.

While fully capable of killing their own fish and rodents, eagles are opportunists looking for an easy meal. Who can blame them? At seven to fourteen pounds eagles are astonishingly light for their size: their hollow bones weigh less than their feathers. But flight consumes so much energy that they must eat 6 to 11 percent of their body weight each day to survive. If a two-hundred-pound man had to eat proportionally as much as an eagle to keep going, he'd consume up to twenty-two pounds of groceries each day. Accordingly, while winter visitors can feast on salmon runs, the resident birds who live when salmon aren't present have to become adept hunters as well.

Bald eagles begin their lives in huge nests that can weigh several hundred pounds. A record-size nest in Florida, built over decades, measured nine and a half feet across and twenty feet deep, and it weighed four thousand pounds. Big nests need big trees, and the fir and cottonwood used for supporting these nests in the Northwest average about thirty inches in diameter at the trunk. When logging has forced Washington's eagles to nest in smaller second-growth trees, the nests have tended to blow down in the winter.

The huge nests are evidence of eagle longevity and stability. Once paired, eagles tend to remain monogamous and will return to the same nest year after year. A typical nest measures about five feet across and three feet deep, and it can be used repeatedly for up to twenty years. Built of sticks, it is lined at the top with grass and other soft material and has a depression about a foot wide to hold the eggs.

As with other birds of prey, the female is larger than the male. Aerial courtship gives way to amour in the nest in which the two caress each other with their beaks as they build up to a brief mating lasting from ten seconds to a minute. The female then lays two to three eggs, each coming about two days apart. For the next thirty-five days the eggs are tirelessly incubated with the parents taking turns. Adults have a patch on their lower breast with blood vessels close to the surface so they can transfer heat to the shells on cold days. The eggs are rotated once an hour. Only three-quarters of the eggs laid ultimately hatch.

When it's time to hatch it can take an eaglet up to two days to break out of its shell. Upon emergence it weighs only three ounces and is so poorly insulated by its down that the parents must warm it at night and shade it by day. The hatchling eats voraciously, and the parents share the exhausting task of providing food. If food is scarce the first-hatched will out-bully his sibling for a meal, starving it to death in nature's grim method of population control. Within two weeks the three-ounce hatchling has grown to two pounds. By the fourth week it is demanding up to two pounds of food per meal. In just two months the eagle has nearly reached adult size.

Their first flight, or fledging, generally occurs at about eighty days. It tends to be as embarrassingly awkward as later flight is smooth. It is difficult for such a big bird to land successfully, and some fledglings tumble ignominiously to the ground. Still, by the end of the summer the young eagles that have survived are self-sufficient. Fewer than half survive, however.

A biologist's rule of thumb is that there must be at least three eaglets hatched each spring, per four nests, for the population to sustain itself or grow. In recent years Washington's eagles have done better than that, averaging more than an eaglet per nest. Accordingly, the population is expanding.

The distinctive white feathers marking sexual maturity do not appear until the eagle is four or five years old. Eagles can live another quarter century in the wild. Given a chance, they are very successful and adaptive raptors, but in a damaged environment, these birds at the top of the food chain quickly pay the cost.

And there's the rub.

Like the spotted owl of old-growth forest fame, the eagle is our harbinger bird, our canary in the coal mine. This is the creature that will first warn us if our environment is about to explode. If we are polluting the landscape, the eagle tends to eat creatures that have concentrated the pollution. If we destroy the other species it dines on, the bell tolls for the eagle as well.

The eagle is a supreme example of why the battle to sustain Pacific Northwest salmon runs is a fight over far more than salmon. If we lose the fish, we'll lose most of the eagles, so important is that massive infusion of ocean protein that eagles dine on at spawning time

As a result, the annual eagle count takes our environmental temperature.

So maybe Ben Franklin was wrong. Maybe the bald eagle *is* the perfect symbol for the American experiment: as fragile as democracy but just as resilient, sensitive to change and yet adaptive as well. It is, in other words, quite a bit like the United States, quite a bit like the Pacific Northwest.

Killer Whales

IN JUST FOUR DECADES THE KILLER WHALE has changed in our perception from monster to environmental icon, from aqua-park sideshow to kidnap victim and movie star—which may say more about us than about the whale.

The tens of thousands of us who rhapsodize while whale-watching around the San Juan Islands each year may not know that in 1956 the U.S. Navy deliberately killed hundreds of orcas in the North Atlantic with machine guns, rockets, and depth charges, ostensibly to aid the Icelandic fishery.

A late as 1964, the Air Force was still using the whales for strafing practice. Canada did the same thing during World War II. In the 1950s, Canadian fisheries authorities mounted a .50-caliber machine gun at the entrance of Johnstone Strait, on the east side of Vancouver Island, in order to shoot if whales approached fishing grounds. (The weapon was never fired.)

The *U.S. Navy Diving Manual* of the 1960s called the killer whale "a ruthless and ferocious beast" and advised divers to leave the water if it was seen. The armed service's *Antarctic Sailing Direction* claimed that the whales "will attack human beings at every opportunity." And of the two hundred and sixty-two orcas captured worldwide between 1962 and 1973, a quarter had gunshot wounds delivered by fishermen and other boaters.

Cut to the dawn of the twenty-first century. Historians can find no evidence of killer whales killing humans. Orcas instead are the darlings of aquarium shows and whale-watching excursions. Millions of dollars are being spent to attempt to re-introduce Keiko, the Newport, Oregon, aquarium star of the movie *Free Willy*, back into the wild off Iceland where he was captured twenty years before.

Nonetheless, this dramatic change in our attitudes is not the most astonishing thing about killer whales. It is instead the fact that individual whales — identifiable animals that can be pointed out by experts in the San Juan Islands — have lived through and survived this period of time, this entire transition of reputation. While birthdates could be off by as much as a dozen years, it is estimated one matriarch dubbed Lummi was born as early as 1910, and Granny in 1911. Males are shorter lived, but Ruffles dates back to 1951.

They've seen us at our gun-wielding, net-capturing worst, have absorbed a century of our pollutants in their blubber, and have lived through a collapse of salmon numbers that has threatened their own clans with hunger. Yet today they will, when the mood strikes them, frolic amidst the boats that come to watch them. I was thrilled, off Whidbey Island, when more than three-dozen whales congregated to socialize playfully around the boat I was on, their black dorsal fins looking like a regatta of dark sailboats tacking this way and that. They breached in twisting corkscrews, slapped the water with fins and tails, and dove under drifting whale-watching boats as if they'd been launched for cetacean amusement. Swimming with easy grace, the whales were pinto beautiful, submarine sleek, and they reeked, when they breathed, of fish.

What were the whales thinking of us when they "spy hopped" vertically out of the water to give us a once over with their liquid dark eye? And what should we think of them, these marine mammals, these gigantic dolphins that stay in family pods for life and seem to have a boundless tolerance for human curiosity?

They are referred to as "killer whales" by Canadian scientists and "orcas" on the politically correct American side

of the border, although the Latin *Orcinus orca* translates anyway as "killer whale." (*Orcinus* means "of the realm of the dead" and *orca* means "whale." The Haida Indians had the same idea as the Romans, calling the mammal *S'gan* for their chief of the underworld.)

And the whales do indeed kill. Rich Osborne, curator at the Friday Harbor Whale Museum, has estimated that the orcas of our resident pods average a take of nearly twenty-five salmon a day each, which means their total consumption, as a group, could be more than eight hundred thousand salmon a year. That's more than sportsmen catch in the same area.

Orcas thrive worldwide, most numerously in colder waters, and were observed and named by the ancient Romans. They have the biggest brain of any mammal on Earth, a mass of gray matter five times larger than ours. "We don't really understand what that big brain is for," says John Ford, a marine mammal scientist at the Vancouver Aquarium. They can see fairly well both above and below water. One captive whale at the Vancouver Aquarium was fascinated by pictures Ford held up to its window of killer whales, yet showed no interest in pictures of other animals. Their distinctive white markings allow us to identify individuals and may help them to do the same.

They have a potential lifespan roughly equal to ours, and take the same number of years that humans do to reach sexual maturity. Males grow to about twenty-three feet in length (the species record is thirty-one and a half feet) and females just under twenty feet. They can weigh three to four tons, and swim up to thirty miles per hour.

Despite their Hollywood "Willy" charm, they are a formidable predator with forty-eight conical teeth and a skull that looks remarkably, Osborne notes, like that of a *Tyranno-*

saurus rex. Those "playful" whales of aquarium shows have nipped, bitten, and nearly drowned some trainers in their off hours. They've been observed harassing dolphins for sport and once spent about two weeks locally playing a game where they pushed dead salmon around with their heads like a ball. Yet killer whales rarely fight each other and have repeatedly shown remarkable restraint when harassed by humans in boats. As predatory as they are, orcas still appear to be a far less violent species than our own.

Washington and British Columbia boast the most intensively studied group of whales in the world, and the most concentrated whale-watching fleet. At the peak a few years ago, more than eighty commercial vessels were taking people to see whales. By 2001, the number was just over sixty.

Tourists are viewing a resident population in the San Juan–Strait of Georgia region that may be in trouble. As of 2001, whale numbers had started an alarming drop to about seventy total, a swift, disturbing decline of nearly twenty animals from their peak in the mid-1990s. Their mean number over the last quarter-century is eighty-four whales.

If the slump is something other than natural variation, whale scientists suspect a combination of circumstances are to blame. They note that K pod presently has no males, possibly hampering reproduction in J and L pods, which rely on neighbor whales to prevent inbreeding. Resident whales are finicky eaters, using salmon for 90 percent of their diet and Chinook for two-thirds of that, and salmon numbers have fallen precipitously. And if hunger strikes, the whales may have to draw on blubber that has stored decades of pollutants (such as PCBs, or polychlorinated biphenyls) passed up the food chain, thereby weakening their immune systems.

In Boundary Bay at the Canadian border, one young

whale, J-18, was found dead of a massive infection. The death may have been linked to an immune system hampered by pollution. "Since PCBs were banned in the 1970s, we're perplexed that we still have such toxic whales," Osborne says. Apparently the chemicals are so persistent in the environment that "the last fifty years of pollution is still in them, just like it is in us."

Transient killer whales that swoop in from the ocean to prey on other marine mammals such as seals have even higher levels of toxins in their blubber. "One of the problems with toxic chemicals is a time lag of up to forty years between the time we clean up our act and top predators become clean," explains David Bain, an animal behavioralist with the University of Washington. Pollutants still being released into the atmosphere in Asia are drifting over the Pacific and raining into the water, where they are absorbed by lower animals that are in turn eaten by bigger ones. Killer whales, at the top of the food chain, absorb the most.

Armadas of whale-watching boats may also increasingly distract whales. When nineteen orcas were trapped in Dyes Inlet for a month in the fall of 1997, the number of sightseeing boats soared as high as five hundred in a single day. Yet usually the whales seem to be capable of ignoring boats when they wish to and playing with them at their whim. "I think they find humans amusing from time to time," Osborne says.

The change in the reputation of orcas from killer to nobility started in 1964 when Samuel Burich, a sculptor, was commissioned by the Vancouver Aquarium to kill a whale in order to fashion a life-size model of it. When he and an assistant harpooned and shot a small one-ton orca, the tough little creature refused to die. Aquarium director Murray Newman decided to tow the feared predator, only fifteen feet long, back to Vancouver. Excited spectators gathered to see a monster long reputed to be as vicious as a great white shark.

The whale surprised everyone by being docile and depressed. Dubbed "Moby Doll," it went on a hunger strike for fifty-five days and died after eighty-seven days in captivity. "It was a nice whale but it was still a predatory, carnivorous creature," Newman insisted to reporters. "It could swallow you alive." To everyone's embarrassment, examination revealed Moby Doll to be Moby Dick: male, not female.

A year later, two fishermen accidentally gillnetted a bull killer whale near Namu, British Columbia. They offered to sell it for eight thousand dollars, and Ted Griffin, owner of the then-private Seattle Aquarium, bought the animal and towed it back in a floating cage. "Namu" created an immediate public sensation. It was like dragging Bigfoot home. Suddenly the hunt was on—every aquarium wanted its own killer whale. Some forty-eight resident whales were captured in local waters and hundreds more were taken worldwide. Yet as the whales proved intelligent and friendly, doubts grew about whale capture.

It ended in Washington State first. In 1976, future Secretary of State Ralph Munro—then an aide to Washington Governor Dan Evans—was sailing off Olympia when he witnessed a whale hunt sponsored by Sea World. Incensed at the harassing tactics, Munro convinced Evans and then–Attorney General Slade Gorton to file suit to block the hunt. Protesters rallied. Children wrote letters. Sea World reaped so much bad publicity over the flap that the Budd Inlet roundup marked the end of the capture era in Puget Sound. Other countries followed suit, with Iceland finally halting captures in 1989.

Meanwhile, in 1974, researcher Michael Bigg had started

to identify individual wild whales in the San Juan Islands by photograph. He found that the number of individuals were fewer than estimated and that their family pods were more tightly knit than suspected. In 1976 Ken Balcomb started a regular orca survey at the Center for Whale Research on San Juan Island, a daily census that still goes on today. As humans turned from capturing to studying the whales, we began to realize just how remarkable these animals are. Their social system is matriarchal, based on their mothers and grand-mothers: male killer whales stay close to the mother their entire life, and the females stay until they have their first calf in their teens. The whales form extended family pods and broader clans, linked by a complex system of calls.

Just as humans live in a world of sight, and many mam-mals such as dogs live in a world of smell, killer whales live in a world of sound. Not only do they use sonar to help find prey, but each pod has a distinctive litany of at least a dozen sounds for communicating. According to John Ford, J pod has been using the same set of calls since listening began in the 1950s. Much of it goes on at high frequencies humans can't easily hear. "They don't have a language the way humans do, but they do communicate with each other," says David Bain. Plans are underway to listen in regularly via a system of hydrophones in Haro Strait.

Sound could help answer pressing questions. Past obser-vations suggest the whales spend about two-thirds of their time foraging for food, 15 percent socializing, and the rest in a rhythmic kind of sleep. However, tracking whales consistently is difficult. We have little idea what they do at night and almost no idea where they go in winter. Scientists were surprised when Northwest "resident" whales showed up offshore at Monterey, California, in the winter.

According to Rich Osborne's charts, K pod migrates into Northwest inland waters as early as March, and L pod joins in June. Typically, L departs around October and K in that month or November, while J stays here, ranging as far south in Puget Sound as Olympia. In summer, the peak feeding and whale-watching time, the pods tend to make a circuit between the mouth of the Fraser River at Vancouver and the Strait of Juan de Fuca, traveling up to a hundred miles a day and swimming through the San Juan Islands to feed on migrating salmon.

A separate group of transient killer whales, numbering one hundred and seventy-four in all, but often visiting individually, swims in from the ocean to prey on seals and sea lions. J pod once chased these interlopers off so aggressively that the transients hid behind a departing ferryboat to get away from their pursuers.

A northern group of two hundred and fifteen orcas is centered on Johnstone Strait farther north along Vancouver Island. Another two hundred and fifty orcas are offshore in the Pacific Northwest. Genetic research by University of British Columbia doctoral student Lance Barrett-Lennard shows that the northern and southern groups are not interbreeding, but the southern group does appear to have some mysterious historical genetic connection to whales in Alaska's Prince William Sound.

Scientists would like to fit some killer whales with tracking devices, but it's illegal and disruptive to capture them to fit anything elaborate. Satellite transmitters used on larger whales are not yet small enough to be reliably fixed to a killer whale's hide with a light crossbow or air rifle.

Osborne says time-depth recorders attached with suction cups have stayed on as long as thirty-six hours before falling off. One finding is that whale-watching has pushed the whales into sleeping less during the day and more at night, with unknown consequences. Another finding is that while orcas spend most of their time near the surface, they occasionally dive to the deepest parts of Puget Sound, hundreds of feet down.

Stomach content analyses of dead whales suggest they are finicky eaters, sticking to a narrow range of prey even if starving. The salmon lovers eat almost exclusively salmon, the seal gourmands eat exclusively seal, and so on.

The research is important because killer whales, like grizzly bears or bald eagles or spotted owls, are at the top of the food chain. Their health relies on the vigor of all the sea animals below them, and thus their population is a barometer of how we're doing as stewards of the environment.

Thus, as killer whales go, so go Northwest waters. "If we can ensure the survival and prosperity of killer whales on this coast," says John Ford, "we can be certain that the underlying marine ecosystem is being preserved." Now the pods show signs of decline, not growth.

There's a disturbing message here. Another species shares the top of the food chain with the killer whale. How long before such ecological decline shows up not just in whales, but in their companion predators?

I refer, of course, to us.

EPILOGUE

A	T THE BEGINNING OF THE BOOK I CALLED you an animal. At its end I'd like to compare you to a virus.

Don't get me wrong! You are quite the astonishing creature. Putting aside the mysterious power of the human brain and your own self-consciousness, your body alone is enough to evoke wonder. You are a walking, thinking, breathing, blood-pumping colony of an estimated hundred trillion cells, or about a thousand times more cells than there are stars in our Milky Way galaxy. Each cell is as complex as a small city, its biological parts corresponding to roads, factories, power plants, storage rooms, and information libraries.

The library is the most extraordinary part. Most cells, not just sperm and egg cells, have a complete coil of DNA that represents the genetic instructions to make another you. The DNA is a chemical text written out in an alphabet of four molecular "letters" that, if typed on pages, would fill several hundred encyclopedia sets. You are a walking set of trillions of instruction manuals, each capable of duplicating you.

Not only is the individual cell an amazing entity in its own right, but your body has "died" and been reborn many times on the cellular level, with old cells expiring and being shed and new ones taking their place, always fitting the master template that makes you *you*. And of course you is quite a you. You don't just run, eat, reproduce, heal, and sleep. You dream, wish, ponder, plot, love, worship, and despair.

As Shakespeare said, what a piece of work is man.

A virus, in comparison, is incredibly simple. It has none of the complexity of even a single cell. It is ten to a hundred times smaller that a typical bacterium. It is not even really alive in any conventional sense of term. It's at that border between life and nonlife, a strip of genetic instructions surrounded by a protein coat that has no more animation than a rock—until it encounters a living thing. Then what is little more than a complex molecule penetrates a host cell, sheds its protein cover, tricks the cell into replicating the viral DNA instead of its own, and usually kills its host in the process. The virus is the ultimate parasite.

Now, a human is not a parasite in the commonly accepted use of the term. We don't fasten onto a single other creature and freeload for our own survival. We actually grow and propagate other species that we need, creating before we consume. Yet we have this similarity to a virus: we are dependent on other living things for our own life. We "come alive" only in partnership with other organisms. We need food. We need oxygen to breathe, and the oxygen on Earth first came from primitive algae. Our breath is sustained by photosynthesis from plants. We are utterly dependent on the ecosystem of our planet.

This dependence is not always obvious. When a Texas billionaire built the domed Biosphere II in the Arizona desert and locked in some human volunteers as an experiment in sustaining an artificial ecosystem, the scientific advisers found they'd overlooked a crucial variable. It wasn't the production of food, though foodstuffs did prove harder to sustain than expected; the Biospherian volunteers lost weight. Still, hunger proved more endurable than the starvation of their lungs. Oxygen! Sure, there were plenty of plants to make it under the enclosed dome. But Biosphere II planners had failed to take adequately into account the trillions upon trillions of microbes that exist in all productive soil. These microscopic creatures didn't produce oxygen, they breathed it; and they breathed in with such vigor that the dome's plants couldn't keep up. Oxygen levels dropped so much that the volunteers found themselves living at the equivalent of high altitude. Under this and other stresses, the ecosystem began to break down, and the one creature that thrived as others disappeared was the ant. The place was overrun by millions and millions of ants.

There's a lesson here. For all our modern achievements, we are ultimately as dependent on other creatures collectively as an inanimate virus is on invading a single cell. The Earth's plants, animals, fungi, and microbes have evolved together to regulate its environment in a self-sustaining way. The ecologist James Lovelock has argued that our planet itself is "alive" in its biological, chemical, and physical processes, and that we interrupt its workings at extreme peril. Astrophysicist John Gribben has gone even further, arguing that not only can we think of the Earth itself as a giant self-regulating organism, but that the Universe too is "alive" in its cyclic creation of stars, their explosive creation of the elements necessary for life, and the violent stellar deaths that distribute those elements to where they can coalesce as new stars, planets, algae, plants, and, ultimately, us. The Universe has evolved to the point where our own planet becomes almost inevitable. It is not just poetry to see the Universe in a flower, it is fact: in the life around us we may be seeing the fundamental truths of existence. In the glimpse of the cougar, the pulse of the jellyfish, the bough of the cedar, we see the sacred. Why else are we so emotionally moved by nature?

So, we sustain the natural order of the Pacific Northwest for at least two reasons. The first is for our survival. The second is for our pleasure, inspiration, worship and a sense of purpose, a sense of being. Cutting ourselves off from our web of life will leave us as dead, physically and spiritually, as an isolated virus. Conversely, if we consume too much we risk consuming our host, dooming ourselves just as a virus can doom itself by attacking its host too vigorously and killing it.

Fortunately, we in this region have the choice of being either a disease or a steward. The Pacific Northwest is unusually blessed. It has a temperate climate. It is well watered. It has a vast variety of landscapes, meaning a rich biodiversity of species. Human numbers are still modest compared to many more-crowded parts of the world, and the people who are here are relatively well educated and well off. We live in a Paradise not quite lost, and we have some small amount of time and room and opportunity to make the changes necessary to keep it.

When I was an environmental and science reporter for the *Seattle Times*, I was struck by how environmentalists and scientists in more troubled and desperate parts of the world looked to this region as exemplary. There were posters in Bangkok and Santiago of our old-growth forests. There was widespread familiarity with our declining salmon runs, curiosity about our regulatory laws. There were calendar pictures of our beauty.

Seen from the perspectives of time and distance, we have

abundant reason for pride and hope. We've preserved many of our best places. We're cleaning our waters. We've improved our handling of waste. Steps, though imperfect, have been taken to corral sprawl. There's a widespread environmental ethic. Many species have made a comeback.

Yet, like the Biospherians, we can take nothing for granted. The list of endangered species is growing, not shrinking. This region loses an estimated thirty thousand to fifty thousand acres of wildlife habitat to human development each year. We've got two centuries of abuses to correct, and a lot of trial and error ahead in fitting our own needs to accord with those of our wild neighbors. Our civilization is so powerful that we're still awkwardly learning how to accommodate it to the planet, lest like a virus we kill what we wish to inhabit. If we kill it, we kill ourselves, morally and biologically.

That's what all the fuss is about.

Are we a virus? Like that simple parasite, we run the risk of becoming some kind of planetary disease. But we are, of course, profoundly different as well. We've got mind and will and hope. Unlike a virus, we also have the free will and ingenuity to become a planetary cure.

I think we shall, just barely. Our knowledge of and commitment to the environment has accelerated enormously in my lifetime. More than that, we have a guide. We're surrounded by neighboring plants and animals that have evolved to fit our environment like a glove. Through their own enduring serenity, their sense of place and perspective, their habits and interactions and mutual interdependence, our neighboring plants and animals of this Northwest are showing us the way.

SUGGESTED READING

WHILE MUCH OF THE INFORMATION FOR this book came from interviews with sources cited in the essays, I also relied heavily on the work of other authors. Readers interested in Pacific Northwest natural history have a wealth of excellent books with which to feed their curiosity. I urge everyone to browse the shelves of a good bookstore or library. The following books are among those I've found most helpful:

Adams, Evelyn. *San Juan Islands Wildlife*. Mountaineers Books, 1995. A guide not just to island species but also to the region itself and the people who care about it. With its own excellent reference guide, reading list, and bibliography.

Alt, David, and Donald Hyndman. *Northwest Exposures: A Geologic History of the Northwest*. Mountain Press, 1995. A compendium of their "roadside" field guides to geology, written in language that laymen can understand.

Arno, Stephen F., and Ramona P. Hammerly. *Northwest Trees: Identifying and Understanding the Region's Native Trees*. Mountaineers Books, 1977. Arno's knowledge is illustrated with Hammerly's exquisite pen-and-ink drawings.

Babcock, Scott, and Bob Carson. *Hiking Washington's Geology*.

Mountaineers Books, 2001. A trail guide with a wealth of accessible information about the ground beneath our feet.

Bodanis, David. *The Secret Garden*. Simon & Schuster, 1992. Utterly fascinating book about the microscopic world of the garden.

Breining, Greg, with Frank Oberle. *Return of the Eagle: How America Saved It's National Symbol*. Falcon Publishing, 1994. A good history, with beautiful photos.

Brown, Greg. *The Great Bear Almanac*. Lyons Press, 1993. A fond look at bears, encyclopedic in scope.

Comins, Neil F. *What If the Moon Didn't Exist?* Harper Collins, 1993. How different our planet would be without its companion satellite! An astronomer speculates on alternative histories of our Earth. Includes a discussion of tides.

Davis, James Luther. *Oregon, Washington, and British Columbia Seasonal Guide to the Natural Year*. Fulcrum Publishing, 1996. Organized by month and place for the species you might see.

Ervin, Keith. *Fragile Majesty: The Battle for North America's Last Great Forest*. Mountaineers Books, 1989. A wealth of natural and human history in a superbly written book by a Northwest journalist. Similar works with different perspectives of time and viewpoint by other journalists include my book *The Final Forest* (Simon & Schuster, 1992), and *Tree Huggers* (Mountaineers Books, 1996) by Kathie Durbin.

Feininger, Andrea. *Trees*. Rizzoli Publications, 1991. An illustrated basic guide to the structure and variety of trees.

Fisher, Chris. *Birds of Seattle and Puget Sound*. Lone Pine Publishing, 1996. A particularly easy-to-use, well-illustrated field guide.

Ford, John K. B., Graeme Ellis, and Kenneth Balcomb. *Killer Whales*. UBC Press and University of Washington Press, 1994. An introduction to the species and a photo guide to individual whales in the San Juans.

Giller, Paul S., and Bjorn Malmqvist. *The Biology of Streams and Rivers.* Oxford University Press, 1998. A wealth of technical information about what goes on in streams.

Gordon, David George. *Field Guide to the Geoduck.* Sasquatch Press, 1996. A good-humored, wonderful introduction to the giant clam. See also Gordon's guides to the bald eagle, the cockroach, and the Sasquatch.

Hillyard, Paul. *The Book of the Spider.* Random House, 1996. A cornucopia of fascinating facts about our eight-legged friends.

Hoyt, Erich. *Orca: The Whale Called Killer.* Camden House Publishing, 1990. A first-person account of whale research. Includes a history of our interactions with the species and much valuable background.

Jensen, Gregory C. *Pacific Coast Crabs and Shrimps.* Sea Challengers Publications, 1992. A field guide by a University of Washington marine biologist and diver who has found several new species in our region's waters.

Kirk, Ruth, with Jerry Franklin. *The Olympic Rain Forest: An Ecological Web.* University of Washington Press, 1992. A well-illustrated primer on forest ecology by an excellent writer and the dean of old-growth research.

Kozloff, Eugene N. *Seashore Life of the Northern Pacific Coast.* University of Washington Press, 1993. A superb guide to six hundred and fifty species by a University of Washington zoologist.

Kruckeberg, Arthur R. *The Natural History of Puget Sound Country.* University of Washington Press, 1991. A comprehensive, well-written, well-illustrated bible to the species, weather, geology, and processes of the Puget Basin.

Langston, Nancy. *Forest Dreams, Forest Nightmares.* University of Washington Press, 1995. A cautionary tale of forest history east of the Cascade Mountains, mentioned here as a great introduction to environmental policy and the perils of human arrogance.

Laskin, David. *Rains All the Time*. Sasquatch Books, 1997. Delightful analysis of Northwest weather for the layman.

Lichatowich, Jim. *Salmon Without Rivers, A History of the Pacific Northwest Salmon Crisis*. Island Press, 1999. Like Langston's book cited above, a cautionary tale of human interaction with the environment.

Logan, William Bryant. *Dirt: The Ecstatic Skin of the Earth*. Riverhead Books, 1995. A poetic exploration of soil. What an unlikely theme, and what a wonderful read.

Love, John A. *Sea Otters*. Fulcrum Publishing, 1992. A great guide to a delightful animal.

Luoma, Jon R. *The Hidden Forest: The Biography of an Ecosystem*. Henry Holt, 1999. A highly readable account of how scientists came to value the ecology of Northwest old-growth forests.

Maser, Chris. *Mammals of the Pacific Northwest*. Oregon State University Press, 1998. A knowledgeable basic guide.

———. *Forest Primeval: The Natural History of an Ancient Forest*. Sierra Club Books, 1989. A thousand-year history of a typical Northwest forest, by one of the region's most outspoken scientists. This is one of several books by Maser on the topic.

Mathews, Daniel. *Cascade-Olympic Natural History: A Trailside Reference*. Raven Editions, 1998. This is the one you want in your backpack, or in the map pocket of your car door.

McNulty, Tim. *Olympic National Park: A Natural History*. Sasquatch Books, 1996. An excellent field guide to the park's plants and animals, from seashore to mountaintop. McNulty has done the same for Mount Rainier. Try his nature poetry: it's great.

Mergen, Bernard. *Snow in America*. Smithsonian Press, 1997. An entire book on snow? Mergen makes the subject fascinating.

Mills, Claudia, and David Wrobel. *Pacific Coast Pelagic Invertebrates*. Sea Challengers, 1998. A field guide to jellyfish, with beautiful photographs.

Nickerson, Roy. *Sea Otters: A Natural History and Guide*. Chronicle Books, 1989. A well-illustrated guide by a journalist. Also includes a history of man-otter interactions.

Norse, Elliott A. *Ancient Forests of the Pacific Northwest*. Island Press, 1990. The argument for saving old growth, expertly told.

Olson, Dennis L. *Cougars: Solitary Spirits*. Northword Press, 1996. Wonderful photographs in a highly readable book about the cats.

Perlin, John. *A Forest Journey: The Role of Wood in the Development of Civilization*. Harvard University Press, 1991. The relationship of people and trees throughout history. Fascinating reading.

Ponting, Clive. *A Green History of the World: The Environment and the Collapse of Great Civilizations*. St. Martin's Press, 1992. If you want practical reasons to care about nature, read this book.

Pyle, Robert Michael. *Wintergreen*. Houghton Mifflin, 1986. An exploration of Washington's Willapa Hills by a butterfly naturalist whose philosophic scope is reminiscent of H. Thoreau or Aldo Leopold. Ramble along also with Pyle's *Chasing Monarchs* and *Where Bigfoot Walks: Crossing the Dark Divide*.

Riedman, Marianne. *Sea Otters*. Monterey Bay Aquarium, 1990. Nicely illustrated layman's guide to a captivating aquatic mammal.

Schenk, George. *Moss Gardening*. Timber Press, 1997. Don't fight it, use it. A book of appreciation by a former Seattle gardener.

Schofield, W. B. *Some Common Mosses of British Columbia*. Royal British Columbia Museum (n.d.). A useful identification guide with valuable background.

Stewart, Hilary. *Cedar: Tree of Life to Northwest Indians*. University of Washington Press, 1995. Eloquent account of how Native Americans used this beautiful tree.

Strickland, Richard. *The Fertile Fjord.* University of Washington Press, 1983 (out of print). An oceanographer's explanation of Puget Sound.

Van Pelt, Robert. *Champion Trees of Washington State.* University of Washington Press, 1996. A fun guide to the big ones.

Vitt, Dale, with Janet Marsh and Robin Bovey. *Mosses, Lichens and Ferns of North America.* Lone Pine Press, 1993. A good background on these often-overlooked plants.

Zwinger, Ann. *The Nearsighted Naturalist.* University of Arizona Press, 1998. A book about seeing the world around us. Thoughtful essays about the environment by an accomplished natural history writer. And just to prove that genes and environment count, her daughter Susan Zwinger, a resident of Whidbey Island, is also an expert nature writer. Read Susan's *The Last Wild Edge.*

INDEX

Actinomycete mold, 27
Adam (Hebrew definition), 70
Admiralty Inlet: depth, 125,
    tidal flow, 129
Alaska: seabird population, 43;
    mosquito population, 99
Alder: use of, 22, 25–26; poi-
    soning of, 22; prevalence of,
    23; seed count, 23; species
    count, 24; ecological role
    of, 25–28; spacing of, 26;
    as animal host, 28; and fire,
    29
Aleut Indians, 49
Anderson, Roland, 185
Animal body plans, 14
Ara-koonen, or Aroughcun
    (origin of term raccoon), 61
Asteroid crash (in Oregon), 124
Astoria, Oregon, 24
Aswan Dam, 73
Audubon, John James, 199

Babylon, and dirt, 73
Bach, Richard, 39–40, 47
Bacteria: number and antiquity
    of, 74, 88
Bain, David, 210, 212
Balcomb, Ken, 212
Bald eagles: range and popu-
    lation, 197; and DDT, 197–
    98, hunting of, 199–200;
    in world culture, 200; in
    antiquity, 200; origin of
    name, 200; migration of,
    201; plumage, 201; courtship,
    202; appetite, 202; nests,
    202–3; life-cycle of, 203–4;
    as environmental warning,
    204
Bambi (film), 30
Barrett-Lennard, Lance, 213
Bay of Fundy, 133
Beattie, Hal, 174
Beecher, Henry Ward, 62

WILLIAM DIETRICH is a staff writer for the
Seattle Times' Pacific Northwest magazine. As a science
reporter for the *Seattle Times*, he won a Pulitzer Prize for
his coverage of the *Exxon Valdez* oil spill. He is the author
of *Northwest Passage: The Great Columbia River* and
*The Final Forest: The Battle for the Last Great Trees of
the Pacific Northwest*, as well as several works of fiction.
He lives in Anacortes, Washington.
Photo © 1998 Eric Droz.

1. Why didn't Dietrich include salmon among the icons of the NW?

2. Did you expect to find chapters on mosquitoes, alder and spiders in such a book?

3. What does the book's title signify to you?

4. What other books would you recommend to someone who enjoyed this one?

5. If you were to add a chapter to this book what topic would you choose?

Keiko & whale watching in SJ's & Dyes Inlet (?
Springer & ?
Arachniphobia
Man/woman hunting cougars
Snow Storm
Clams & Crabs
Eagles & Otters on B.I.
Park Institute & Elder Hostel Courses